FUTURESCAN

Health Care Trends and Implications

2022–2027

T0336458

The U.S. Health Care System as It Emerges from a Pandemic

by Ian Morrison, PhD

The COVID-19 pandemic has created massive changes in the U.S. health care system, stressing institutions, the workforce and individual caregivers. But it has also spurred lasting permanent change, including a profound shift to digital solutions, increased awareness of inequities, exposure of weaknesses in financing models, massive pressure on the workforce, recognition of the need for more effective integration of physical and mental health in policy and practice, and the imperative for improved emergency preparedness.

This edition of *Futurescan* draws on the subject matter expertise of eight of the nation's top health leaders to synthesize key trends that will shape health care in a post-pandemic world.

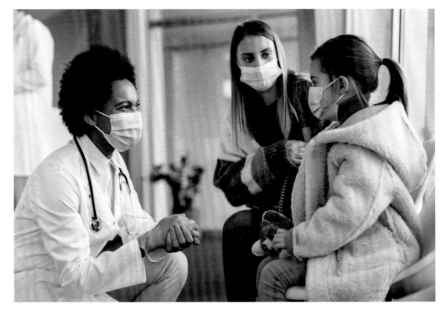

Care Transformation

Michael Dowling, president and CEO of Northwell Health, draws on his vast experience and leadership in the eye of the storm of the pandemic to distill enduring lessons of change. He believes that one of the most transformative overarching trends—the rise of consumerism in health care—will only accelerate in the post-COVID environment. Yet regulatory burdens have made transformation difficult. "Health systems need the freedom to transform based on the customer's perspective," Dowling states. "That has not traditionally been the case, however, as the formation or mergers of large health systems are frequently blocked or challenged by local and federal regulators."

Consumer-facing technology is just one area that health care executives should consider developing. Pricing transparency also has become especially important in an environment where many Americans have lost their jobs, and thus their health insurance.

Dowling urges health system leaders to take the experience of the pandemic to focus on the future, offering several suggestions for actualizing change:

- Focus on consumerism and the customer experience.
- Invest in technology infrastructure.
- Advocate for easing regulatory burdens.
- Focus on care outside the walls of the hospital.

Workforce

Catherine A. Jacobson, president and CEO of Froedtert Health, is a national leader in highlighting the workforce challenges that hospital and health system

About the Author

Ian Morrison, PhD, is an author, consultant and futurist. He received an undergraduate degree from the University of Edinburgh, Scotland; a graduate degree from the University of Newcastle upon Tyne, England; and an interdisciplinary doctorate in urban studies from the University of British Columbia, Canada. He is the author of several books, including the best-selling *The Second Curve: Managing the Velocity of Change*. Morrison is the former president of the Institute for the Future and a founding partner of Strategic Health Perspectives, a forecasting service for clients in the health care industry.

executives face. Even before the pandemic, workforce issues were emerging across the operational and clinical spectrum. Burnout among clinicians was reaching crisis proportions, and COVID-19 only magnified the stress and fatigue felt by health care workers. At the same time, health care was experiencing shifts in workflow and workforce requirements because of new technologies and different types of care delivery. The pandemic accelerated these shifts dramatically in that, over a matter of weeks, many hospital employees were operating in crisis mode.

The social unrest that spotlighted racial inequities later in 2020, combined with the higher COVID-19 infection and mortality rates among people of color, underscored the need for employers to examine their own response to these issues.

Over the next five years, Jacobson urges health system leaders to focus on several workforce issues that have risen to greater prominence in the wake of COVID-19:

- Facilitating mental well-being.
- Fostering leadership development.
- Reengineering the workforce.
- Erasing racial bias and inequities in care and employment.

Strategy

Kenneth Kaufman is managing director and chair of health care consulting firm Kaufman Hall, and one of the leading thinkers on the future of health care. The COVID-19 reset of the U.S. economy will reverberate well beyond the end of the pandemic, Kaufman predicts. Every hospital and health system is being challenged to understand how this economic restart is creating competitive stressors and how organizations need to react.

For health care organizations, the critical question is to what extent the business model and nature of competition in health care will be based more on technology and less on face-to-face care delivery. Assuming a continued strong demand for virtual care, hospital and health system executives need to think of competition broadly in two new ways:

- The extent to which tech companies will continue to encroach on the space of traditional providers.

- How to improve digital offerings as the basis of market competition shifts to greater digital sophistication.

What is needed is not just a review of competitive strategy. Rather, Kaufman says, "Competitive strategy must be informed by a new thought process shaped to confront an economic and competitive environment that, accelerated by the pandemic, is in the process of changing forever."

Health Equity

Juana S. Slade, chief diversity officer and director of language services at not-for-profit health system AnMed Health in South Carolina and Northeast Georgia, has been leading efforts to foster inclusion and diversity for more than 20 years. She asserts that by any measure, 2020 was a pivotal year that sparked a national reexamination of social injustice, racial bias and health inequities.

Related to these issues are the realities of how social determinants of health impact clinical outcomes. Diversity has become a new imperative, along with cultural competence and the ability of providers to effectively deliver health care services that meet the social, cultural and linguistic needs of patients.

At AnMed, Slade has demonstrated that a health system can make great strides in addressing racial bias and health inequities. She recommends the following strategies:

- Develop a diverse organization.
- Foster cultural competence.
- Influence and invest in the community.

Finance

David Blumenthal, MD, HFACHE, is president of The Commonwealth Fund and a renowned health services researcher and national authority on health information technology adoption. As the nation continues to struggle with the economic effects of COVID-19, Blumenthal shares his thoughts on the likely reimbursement outlook for government payers and commercial insurers over the next five years.

Public insurance programs are likely to grow as the Biden administration moves to make the health insurance marketplace more accessible and the Medicaid program more available to eligible Americans. Value-based care will be emphasized, predicts Blumenthal.

Meanwhile, the pandemic may have lingering effects on commercial insurers. Provider consolidations may gather momentum as weak medical practices and financially challenged hospitals look to align with more sustainable institutions.

Financial incentives are still not properly aligned to drive value-based care, Blumenthal observes. However, external pressures may continue to move health care reimbursement toward prospective payment models.

Virtual Health

Randy D. Oostra, DM, FACHE, CEO of the not-for-profit ProMedica health system, maintains that telemedicine may be the most prevalent form of virtual health but will soon be far from the only one. Oostra says a lot of innovation and consumer acceptance has happened in a very short period of time. He predicts rapid and widespread adoption of a variety of virtual health business models by players both inside and outside legacy health care systems.

Oostra says health system executives will want to weigh several issues when considering virtual health offerings, including:

- Capital investments.
- Impact on providers.
- Impact on social determinants of health.

He offers the following advice for hospital executives:

- View patients as consumers.
- Reevaluate investments in brick and mortar.
- Consider how to deliver current services in nontraditional ways.
- Evaluate the costs.
- Look for collaborators instead of building new virtual health services.

Behavioral Health

Harsh K. Trivedi, MD, is president and CEO of Sheppard Pratt, the nation's largest private, not-for-profit provider of mental health, substance use, developmental disability, special education and social services. Trivedi says behavioral health services have been undervalued and underfunded for many years. COVID-19 had a negative impact on an already-tenuous mental health safety net, and hospitals are feeling the effects in several ways.

The pandemic has made behavioral health services even more necessary than ever before. Considerable evidence suggests that addressing behavioral health issues in a collaborative care model with primary care yields significantly better outcomes and lowers overall costs. As the country's health care system moves toward value-based care, greater investment in behavioral health services is needed.

Trivedi suggests several strategies for fortifying an existing mental health services continuum in the post-COVID environment:

- Develop the behavioral health infrastructure.
- Create linkages with providers who are already in this space.
- Embrace telehealth.

Emergency Preparedness

Gregory R. Ciottone, MD, is president of the World Association for Disaster and Emergency Medicine and a disaster medicine expert. "Because of COVID-19, we gained a greater understanding of the complexities of disasters," Ciottone states. But, he cautions, "The pandemic has also underscored that we need to pay more attention to emergency preparedness. . . . To prepare for the next global health crisis, we need to determine more proactively how complex disasters are best mitigated."

In the world of emergency preparedness, 75 percent of the time and effort is spent in the mitigation, preparedness and recovery phases, rather than in the emergency response itself. Hospitals need to be continually engaged in mitigating, preparing for and responding to complex disasters. Ciottone recommends the following actions:

- Teach crisis leadership skills.
- Ensure every internal department understands its role in a disaster.
- Maintain relationships with other first responders in the community.
- Establish close linkages with public health agencies to enhance communication and interagency cooperation.
- Consider the psychological toll of disasters on health care workers.

Conclusion

COVID-19 has wreaked havoc on health care but has also spurred leaders to respond creatively to the challenges they have faced over the past two years. They have learned enduring lessons, including the need to pivot to digital health, to focus on workforce resilience, to respond creatively in crisis, to integrate behavioral and mental health, to foster diversity and inclusion, and to address the inevitable competition from big tech and big retail as Apple, Amazon, Google and Facebook strengthen their positions in the multitrillion-dollar U.S. health care system. Winners in the future will harness technology to meet consumers and communities where they live while also preserving and enhancing the work–life balance of the clinicians who serve them in the face of increasing uncertainty and danger. The many thoughtful contributions in this edition of *Futurescan* will benefit health care leaders and help guide their strategic priorities in the years ahead.

The Post-COVID Transformation of Health Care Delivery

with Michael Dowling

Before COVID-19, several key trends had been gaining momentum in the transformation of health care delivery. The pandemic greatly magnified those developments, according to Michael Dowling, president and CEO of Northwell Health. Dowling leads New York's largest health system with 22 hospitals, a vast ambulatory care network, home care services and more. He believes that one of the most transformative overarching trends—the rise of consumerism in health care—will only accelerate in the post-COVID environment.

"C-suite executives need to recognize that health care is a service industry," Dowling says. "Patients today are different than they were 20 years ago. They have more knowledge and access to technology, which they use to compare prices, convenience, services and more." Consumers have different standards for quality than what providers assume, Dowling notes. "What our health care customers want is kindness, punctuality, easy access and friendly staff. Quality is assumed."

The COVID-19 pandemic motivated many consumers to make different health care choices. The percentage of patients who postponed needed care rose from about 22 percent in the first quarter of 2020 to more than 30 percent in the second quarter (NRC Health 2021). The COVID-19 pandemic also greatly accelerated consumers' acceptance of telehealth; the number of virtual visits was 50 percent higher during the first three months of 2020 than during the same period in 2019 (Koonin et al. 2020). Furthermore, telemedicine was extremely successful: 92 percent of patients surveyed about more than 150,000 telehealth encounters reported positive sentiments about their experience. Nearly two-thirds of respondents in another survey said they would be willing to use virtual care in the future (PwC 2021).

Clearly, the rise in consumerism is a monumental shift in how health care buying decisions are made, and consumerism will become critical in the future. "The single most important distinguishing characteristic of successful health care organizations post-COVID will be service," Dowling asserts. Other trends will make health care delivery different over the next five years, and Dowling explains what health care executives should do to prepare.

About the Subject Matter Expert

Michael Dowling is one of health care's most influential voices, taking a stand on societal issues that many health system CEOs shy away from, such as gun violence and immigration. As president and CEO of Northwell Health, he leads a clinical, academic and research enterprise with a workforce of more than 76,000 and annual revenues of $14 billion. Dowling chairs the Institute for Healthcare Improvement board of directors and has received numerous awards, including the Ellis Island Medal of Honor and honorary degrees from Fordham University, University College Dublin in Ireland and the prestigious Queen's University Belfast. Prior to joining Northwell in 1995, Dowling served in New York State government for 12 years and as a chief adviser to former Governor Mario Cuomo.

FUTURESCAN SURVEY RESULTS
Care Transformation

Health care executives from across the nation were asked how likely it is that the following will happen in their hospital or health system by 2027.

By 2027, our hospital or health system will have expanded its electronic medical record system to incorporate 100 percent of data from individuals' health care experiences, including inpatient and subacute settings.

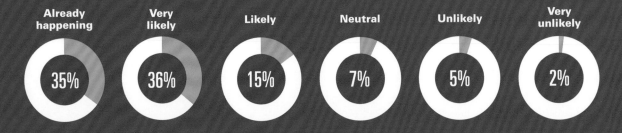

Already happening	Very likely	Likely	Neutral	Unlikely	Very unlikely
35%	36%	15%	7%	5%	2%

By 2027, our hospital or health system will have increased its investment in digital consumer strategies by at least 20 percent (e.g., use of a digital front door, integrated patient portal, and highly customized communication with individuals).

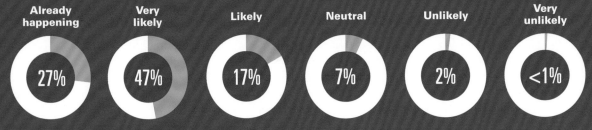

Already happening	Very likely	Likely	Neutral	Unlikely	Very unlikely
27%	47%	17%	7%	2%	<1%

Note: Percentages may not sum exactly to 100 percent because of rounding.

Implications for Health Care Leaders

Although the COVID-19 pandemic changed how many consumers access health care, it also created a fundamental need for innovation in provider organizations. Many health systems rose to the occasion by using new technology and creating novel modes of service delivery. Government agencies facilitated these changes by easing restrictions and allowing hospitals to increase bed capacities, create new specialized patient care units, implement crisis standards of care and more. Dowling says that the need to transform service delivery will be even greater as health care moves beyond the four walls of the hospital to community-based points of care (exhibit 1). He urges health care leaders to consider the following imperatives and their potential impacts over the next few years.

Technology's role in care transformation. Health systems have invested heavily in clinical and information technology to deliver and document care provided to patients. However, many health systems need to make further investments in consumer-facing technologies that enhance convenience and communication with providers, streamline access to electronic health information and improve the overall customer experience. One platform that meets all three objectives is Playback Health, a cloud-based app that answers the question "What did the doctor say?"

Northwell's partnership with Playback Health enables the system's providers to create personalized videos with patient-specific health information and directives regarding preoperative

Exhibit 1

Creating a Platform for Consumers to Seek Health and Experience Wellness

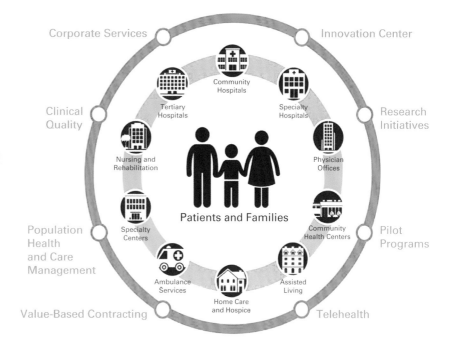

preparation, test results, post-discharge medications and more. The videos are uploaded to Playback Health in the cloud for patients and families to access using their mobile devices. During the pandemic, Northwell used Playback Health to close the communication gap with family members who were not allowed to visit loved ones in the hospital. Clinicians posted videos on the patients' condition status, treatment plan and any other information the family needed to know. Family members can replay the videos as often as necessary to keep abreast of patient status and to confirm their understanding of current treatments. The videos become an unofficial but portable medical record.

UPMC, headquartered in Pittsburgh, Pennsylvania, worked with vendor-partner Certify to use biometric technology to expedite the patient experience

at hospital campuses and physician practices throughout the system of more than 40 hospitals. Patients can check in during the registration process with the mere touch of an index finger. With more than a million fingerprints captured to date, the organization is not only creating a personalized patient experience but also preventing identity theft and fraud and enhancing patient safety. UPMC also worked with Certify to adapt facial recognition technology during the COVID-19 pandemic to capture more than 16 million digital temperature scans at all hospital entrances.

Deborah Heart and Lung Center in Browns Mills, New Jersey, is using two innovations to help patients manage their medications. Shortly after discharge, an automated text message is sent to patients' cell phones with educational information about the medications they

have been prescribed, locations of nearby pharmacies and, if available, discounted pricing on certain drugs. The feedback on this system has been overwhelmingly positive, with more than 90 percent of participating patients expressing approval. Deborah also uses software that assists physicians in writing patient prescriptions at the time of discharge. When a prescription is ready to be created in the electronic health record, a real-time benefits check estimates the cost to patients based on their insurance plan and pharmacy, and alternative medications and pharmacies are listed if the initial prescription is cost prohibitive. The software helps to ensure patient compliance because doctors are not otherwise aware of the cost to patients when they prescribe medications.

Pricing transparency. In an environment where more Americans have

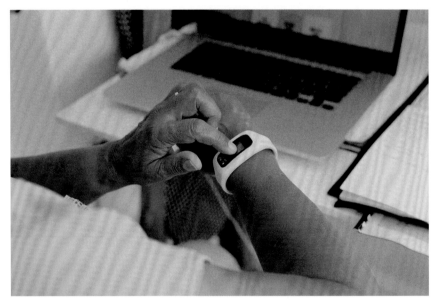

challenged by local and federal regulators." The pandemic showed the rapidity with which federal, state and local agencies can respond to changing health care needs in the midst of a national emergency. The easing of licensing restrictions, adoption of crisis standards of care, increased funding for telehealth and rapid turnaround of Food and Drug Administration approvals on vaccines and treatments all demonstrated that the government can change course when needed.

Action Steps for Health Care Leaders

Dowling recommends the following strategies in the wake of the COVID-19 pandemic.

Focus on consumerism and the customer experience. The pandemic has been a seminal event in terms of consumerism. In 2020, 36 percent of consumers had no preference for a health care brand, and 62 percent expected that whatever preference they had would change after COVID-19. Furthermore, 49 percent reported that convenience was a primary driver in their health care decision-making, and 52 percent said convenience was their second-most important criterion for brand preference (NRC Health 2021). Clearly, providing easy access is crucial to attracting care-seeking consumers.

Another key differential gaining in importance is the ability of consumers to estimate their out-of-pocket expenses on a provider's website based on insurance and diagnosis. Dowling believes that access to and portability of medical records via patient portals will also become a standard expectation among consumers.

Invest in technology infrastructure. Without question, digital strategies will become integral to serving consumers over the next five years. From online scheduling, texted appointment reminders and virtual check-in to the collection of health data online or via wearable technology, consumers are

lost their jobs, and thus their health insurance, than at any other time in recent memory, pricing transparency has become especially important. Before they book a health care interaction, patients want to know what their out-of-pocket expense will be. And it is not just desirable for providers to convey the cost per procedure by insurer—it is now mandatory. Starting January 1, 2021, hospitals have been required to post payer-negotiated rates for common services online in a consumer-friendly format.

Systemness. COVID-19 demonstrated that hospitals are only one link in a long chain needed to effectively manage patients, especially in a crisis. The pandemic showed that hospitals cannot operate alone. "It was because of our systemness that Northwell never saw a shortage of personal protective equipment, beds, ventilators or staff in areas of need," Dowling notes. "Hospitals that span locations and operate

as a holistic ecosystem are inherently prepared to support one another in the face of a prolonged natural or manmade disaster."

Transforming care outside the hospital. "In reality, the majority of health care services are not provided in the hospital setting," Dowling observes. This trend will accelerate in the future as a result of technological and clinical advances, to the point where hospitals become facilities that primarily treat patients with intensive care needs. More care will be delivered in the home to support patients who want—and are able—to age in place.

Innovation in care delivery. "Health systems need the freedom to transform based on the customer's perspective," Dowling states. "That has not traditionally been the case, however, as the formation or mergers of large health systems are frequently blocked or

Consumers have embraced a new era of access to medical care, using technology and demanding a streamlined customer experience.

primed for digital-first encounters before they even see their clinicians. Most health care executives responding to the latest *Futurescan* survey are already tracking with this development: 91 percent said their organization is already engaged or likely to engage in digital consumer strategy investments.

Conversa is one example of a virtual care and triage platform that uses self-generated health data, such as symptoms and biometrics, to identify at-risk patients and provide highly personalized, automated recommendations on where next to seek care, if indicated. Conversa's chatbot is powered by artificial intelligence and relies on an extensive library of evidence-based virtual care pathways to help patients manage chronic disease, perioperative care, post-discharge care, medication adherence, pregnancy, wellness and more. Using Conversa's COVID-19 HealthCheck, a screening tool for coronavirus disease, Northwell established a testing initiative in faith-based communities to ensure people in underserved areas are able to find out whether they are or have been infected. Working in collaboration with the New York State Department of Health and local faith leaders, Northwell provided more than 85,000 free diagnostic and antibody tests in over a hundred locations across metropolitan New York and vaccinated more than 41,000 individuals in 52 neighborhood and faith-based locations in communities of color from January to May 2021.

Advocate for easing regulatory burdens. Continuing to ease restrictions in the wake of COVID-19 will allow health systems to transform care through innovations. Dowling urges health care leaders to use their influence to advocate for freedom in responding to marketplace trends that benefit consumers. Two areas in particular have far-reaching ramifications:

- **Certificate-of-need applications.** Governments often mandate how different spaces inside hospitals

and nursing homes can be used. Current approaches to analyzing the advantages of health system development fail to recognize the tangible benefits a community experiences by having access to a coordinated, integrated platform to deliver health care and promote health. During the pandemic, however, New York State allowed hospitals to implement surge plans by waiving the requirement for elaborate certificate-of-need applications that normally must be completed by hospitals wanting to expand their footprint or services. As a result, bed capacity increased as much as 50 percent. "COVID-19 demonstrated that large health systems can quickly pivot in response to a public health crisis," Dowling states. "The suspension of low-value regulatory burdens not only gave health systems greater agility but also supported innovation in patient care, staffing and facility utilization. The regulatory framework needs to be revisited and streamlined to recognize the benefits of health system formation."

- **Telehealth.** Soon after the pandemic struck, the New York State Department of Financial Services followed the lead of the U.S. Centers for Medicare & Medicaid Services and declared that insurance plans

should pay for telehealth visits at the same rates as for in-person visits. Between March 1, 2020, and May 6, 2021, Northwell caregivers conducted more than 523,300 remote patient visits, including nearly 369,100 video consultations. Telehealth has proven to be a good alternative for those who need ongoing care for chronic medical issues but are unwilling or unable to travel to their doctor's office. Many consumers who prefer the convenience of a virtual consultation now clearly expect remote visits to be an option.

Focus on care outside the hospital walls. Health systems should consider creating or investing in strong partnerships in sites across the full continuum of care, including community-based clinics, specialty centers, post-acute and rehabilitation settings, nursing homes, home care and hospice services, and more. With the rapid adoption of telehealth during the pandemic, consumers have also become more accustomed to interfacing with clinicians in their own homes. One study found that 75 percent of patients are willing to receive care at home for an illness or injury, chronic condition or wellness visit (PwC 2021). The hospital-at-home model, while still in its early stages, has the potential for widespread consumer acceptance.

Conclusion

The COVID-19 pandemic will have lasting effects on the American health care system. Consumers have embraced a new era of access to medical care, using technology and demanding a streamlined customer experience—much of it delivered outside the hospital's four walls.

"By addressing the issues that have come to light in the aftermath of the pandemic and assimilating the lessons learned and still-emerging solutions," Dowling asserts, "health care executives can position their enterprises for success over the long term, before the next national emergency."

References

Koonin, L., B. Hoots, C.A. Tsang, Z. Leroy, K. Farris, B. Tilman Jolly, P. Antall, B. McCabe, C.B.R. Zelis, I. Tong and A.M. Harris. 2020. "Trends in the Use of Telehealth During the Emergence of the COVID-19 Pandemic—United States, January–March 2020." *Morbidity and Mortality Weekly Report.* Published October 30. www.cdc.gov/mmwr/volumes/69/wr/mm6943a3.htm.

NRC Health. 2021. *NRC Health 2021 Healthcare Consumer Trends Report.* Accessed July 5. https://nrchealth.com/wp-content/uploads/2021/01/NRC-Health-2021-Healthcare-Consumer-Trends-Report.pdf.

PwC. 2021. *Consumer Health Behavior and the COVID-19 Pandemic: What We've Learned.* Published April. www.pwc.com/us/en/industries/health-industries/library/assets/hri-2021-consumer-survey-Insight-chartpack.pdf.

Evolving Workforce Priorities in the Wake of the Pandemic

with Catherine A. Jacobson

Prior to 2020, health system executives were becoming concerned about workforce issues emerging in a variety of areas across the operational and clinical spectrum. The incidence of burnout among clinicians, which manifested as depression, anxiety, post-traumatic stress syndrome and suicidal ideation, was reaching crisis proportions. When COVID-19 became a national pandemic, it magnified the stress and fatigue felt by health care workers at all levels of the organization. It also changed their workflow dramatically—in a matter of weeks, many hospital employees were operating in crisis mode.

Catherine A. Jacobson, president and CEO of Froedtert Health in Wisconsin, is one of the health care executives who had been leading the national discussion on the challenges facing health care workers and the organizations that employ them. "Before the coronavirus pandemic, resilience and the mental well-being of physicians, providers and employees had risen to the top of the agenda for many health system leaders," Jacobson says. "The pandemic catapulted the stress and anxiety to a much higher level and took a traumatic toll on the entire health care workforce. The long hours, the unyielding surge in patients, shortages of personal protective

equipment and ventilators, and the death toll all made for battlefield-like conditions."

The social unrest that spotlighted racial inequities later in the year, combined with the higher COVID-19 infection and mortality rates among people of color, underscored the need for employers to examine their own response to these issues. "All of these stressors continue to impact health care across the country and have permanently changed care delivery and the conditions under which many employees work," Jacobson asserts.

Key Challenges Facing the Health Care Field

According to Jacobson, three critical workforce concerns continue to evolve in the wake of the pandemic.

Behavioral health issues. In addition to amplifying the stress and workload of health care workers, the COVID-19 pandemic introduced a pervasive sense of uncertainty and fear. The high infection and mortality rates, lack of access to effective treatments, isolation of the sick from their families, disparities seen in communities of color and fear of

About the Subject Matter Expert

Catherine A. Jacobson is president and CEO of Froedtert Health, a regional health care system based in Milwaukee, Wisconsin. Jacobson joined Froedtert Health in 2010 as executive vice president of finance and strategy, chief financial officer and chief strategy officer. She was promoted to president in 2011 and assumed the CEO role in 2012. Prior to joining Froedtert Health, Jacobson spent 22 years at Rush University Medical Center in Chicago in various leadership roles. Jacobson is a certified public accountant. She received her bachelor of science degree in accounting from Bradley University in Peoria, Illinois.

Health care executives from across the nation were asked how likely it is that the following will happen in their hospital or health system by 2027.

By 2027, as compared to today's levels, our hospital or health system will have reduced clinicians' administrative tasks by at least 30 percent.

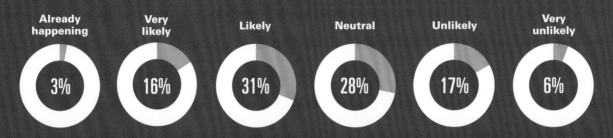

Already happening	Very likely	Likely	Neutral	Unlikely	Very unlikely
3%	16%	31%	28%	17%	6%

By 2027, our hospital or health system will have multiple partnerships/collaborations to increase the diversity of its workforce (e.g., by collaborating with local community agencies to train people for health care careers).

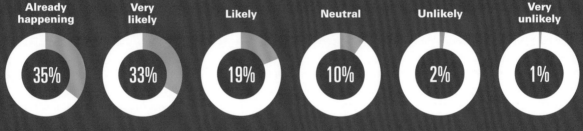

Already happening	Very likely	Likely	Neutral	Unlikely	Very unlikely
35%	33%	19%	10%	2%	1%

Note: Percentages may not sum exactly to 100 percent because of rounding.

contracting the virus or passing it on to loved ones was traumatically stressful among hospital workers across the country. The pressures were not limited to the work environment, as many employees had to deal with children home from school, spouses laid off or underemployed, and family members who became ill or passed away. It was unavoidable that these stressors manifested within the work enviroment. Even though the infection rates have declined, many states are still feeling the aftereffects of COVID-19.

Impact of technology. Health care is experiencing concurrent shifts in workflow and workforce requirements because of new technology and the need for different types of care delivery. For instance, the rapid and widespread adoption of telehealth during the pandemic radically changed how physician visits are conducted and diminished the need for support staff. Before March 2020, fewer than 1 percent of health care visits at the Froedtert & the Medical College of Wisconsin health network were completed via telehealth; by the end of 2020, telehealth accounted for approximately 25 percent of all medical visits, and the trend is predicted to grow. Technology continues to streamline and automate systems, requiring fewer employees and staff members with different skill sets. These advances will require retraining and redeploying personnel. In some areas, a shortage of skilled workers may change how employees are recruited and trained.

Racial inequities. As social protests mounted in 2020, racism and health inequities continued to affect the health, safety and livelihoods of people of color. Employees from racial and ethnic minority groups still coexist with these inequities every day. Systemic bias that is endemic in the employment setting often perpetuates discrimination. Health system executives must formulate strategies to address racial inequities in hiring practices, leadership and personnel policies, and procedures across the enterprise.

Implications for Health Care Leaders

Over the next five years, Jacobson urges health system leaders to focus on several workforce issues that have risen to greater prominence in the wake of COVID-19.

Facilitating mental well-being. Jacobson says that employee wellness must remain a top priority for health care executives over the next five years. Some organizations were already developing initiatives around this strategy before the pandemic struck. HealthPartners in Bloomington, Minnesota, recognized the importance of workforce mental well-being when it established its Center for Employee Resilience in 2018. The center provides support for employees whose work is challenging and demanding, physically and emotionally. The center is spacious, with large windows, natural light, comfortable chairs and tools for calming restoration. It offers weekly classes on meditation, gentle yoga, group mindfulness and more.

One-on-one resilience coaching is provided free of charge and helps employees discover, crystallize and align their goals with the support of a board-certified wellness coach. Customized team resilience training is also conducted, based on the needs of each work group. During the pandemic, nursing units with a high number of COVID-19 patients supported the resilience of their teams by partnering with on-site wellness instructors and creating a resilience room on their floor. In 2020, HealthPartners launched MentalHealth@Work, a psychotherapy clinic that offers convenient on-site and video appointments with a licensed mental health provider to support employees and their mental health needs.

Mount Sinai Health System was greatly impacted by the surge of COVID-19 patients in New York in March 2020. The pandemic accelerated

the creation of a concept that director of rehabilitation innovation David Putrino, PhD, had been developing for some time: Recharge Rooms, a place where staff can enter a physiologically calming environment. "We use a scientific, evidence-based approach and biophilic principles to connect visitors to the natural world, with projectors showing scenes of nature, aromatherapy, plants, soft responsive lighting and soundscaped music," Putrino explains. "For 10 minutes, each staff person can enjoy passive stress release that brings their physiology down."

Putrino says the initial build-out included four Recharge Rooms. Within three months, 13,000 employees had visited the rooms and had lodged requests for similar spaces closer to their units. The concept was so successful that the health system created 20 more Recharge Rooms, located across all eight hospitals. "We often think of resilience as a personal trait, but I think of it more

as a resource," Putrino notes. "If someone feels they are accepted and safe and others care about their well-being, that sense brings its own resilience in even the most difficult circumstances."

Physician burnout has been a problem in health care since before the pandemic. Gundersen Health System in Wisconsin decided to address the issue in 2018. Pediatric cardiologist Susan G. Maclellan-Tobert, MD, FACC, explains: "We took a boots-to-the-ground approach and developed an internal coaching program for our peers. Clinicians are already high functioning and resilient, *and* we are challenged daily by stress, workload and energy-draining activities. So how can we become our best selves and continue to thrive in a challenging work environment? We believe peers helping peers to grow in resilience and self-care is the key." After completing a six-month certified physician development program that provided training specific to coaching

The rapid and widespread adoption of telehealth during the pandemic radically changed how physician visits are conducted.

physicians, Maclellan-Tobert and two other clinicians launched Gundersen's peer coaching program in June 2019. Coaching is provided on an individual or group basis.

"Medical school emphasizes putting the patient first, sometimes to the detriment of the clinician's well-being," she says. "We want our peers to know that building resilience is about expanding the well of inner resources that allow you to face the daily challenges of being a clinician." One program offering is a comprehensive eight-session course on building resilience, but individual coaching is otherwise personalized to every clinician to promote introspection, personal growth and self-awareness. To date, more than 60 clinicians have availed themselves of the program. When departmental coaching was introduced in 2019, the physician burnout rate in one department decreased from 72 percent to 39 percent. During the COVID-19 pandemic, Gundersen's peer coaches offered "virtual lounges" to clinicians to help them manage stress. "Immediately, three groups popped up to help our clinicians connect with one another and move through the pandemic together," Maclellan-Tobert says. When the groups finished in spring 2021, it was a testimonial to how Gundersen's coaches had equipped their peers to handle the stress.

Leadership development. Training on managing through a crisis, in particular, will be key. Johns Hopkins Medicine developed a unique curriculum called Frontline Crisis Leadership in direct response to the COVID-19 pandemic. It is based largely on the expertise of George S. Everly Jr., PhD, who developed the Johns Hopkins RAPID Psychological First Aid methodology and is an expert in disaster psychology. "We were asked to create a plan to address the psychological effects on our staff of working through COVID, knowing there would be a great deal of stress and burnout," says Carolyn Cumpsty Fowler, senior director for nursing well-being at the Johns Hopkins Medicine Office of Well-Being. Cumpsty Fowler codeveloped and deployed the Frontline Crisis Leadership program with Everly and a core group of experts. "During a crisis, managers need to lead differently," she notes. "They need to pay more attention to psychological well-being, not 'how we are doing.' Leaders often try to problem-solve, but employees have complex lives. Our curriculum provides four pillars and 10 basic principles that help leaders reduce psychological casualties during a short- or long-term crisis."

The one-hour training program was introduced in May 2020 to senior health system leaders, nurse managers, department directors and advanced practice personnel. Requests were quickly received for additional training from departments across the organization. "People appreciate the opportunity to have this conversation," notes Cumpsty Fowler. "Well-being and self-care need to be embedded in the workplace, before the next crisis occurs."

Reengineering the workforce. Workforce requirements over the next five years will lead to the consolidation or elimination of some types of positions, along with the creation of new ones. As a result, health care executives may want to revisit their staff development plans. "We have seen shortages of some skilled and even lower-wage workers," notes Jacobson. Froedtert was the first health system in the region to implement a $15 minimum wage to retain its labor force, which led to pay raises for more than 6,500 staff members. "We also anticipate the need to re-skill current team members," she says. "For instance, operating room technicians are in short supply in Froedtert's marketplace. We are exploring 'growing' our own workforce through internal training programs, partnering with outside schools to train needed technicians and clinicians. Recently, we established an $11.5 million scholarship program for underprivileged and deserving students to help address these staffing needs and social determinants of health such as education and employment." In some cases, the health system is paying workers to do their jobs and attend school as well. Loan forgiveness is offered to some hard-to-find professionals.

The pandemic may also have permanently altered some workflows. For example, virtual visits do not require frontline staff to book appointments or to room patients. Without the need for these employees, the health system has been able to add medical assistants who allow registered nurses to work at the top of their license, a staffing strategy that was critical during the surge in COVID-19 patients. "We do not have enough people to do the jobs we need done," Jacobson observes. "We're learning how to deliver health care with fewer people, or hiring different people over the long term."

Erasing racial bias and inequities.
Eradicating inequities and racism will be integral to meeting the needs of all employees, as well as the diverse populations every health system serves. "We have an obligation to reflect the community in our workforce," Jacobson states. Froedtert Health's Eradicating Racism and Enhancing Health Equity plan is an expansive, multitrack initiative aimed at eliminating bias, building workforce diversity, ensuring health equity and supporting communities of color while driving change to help end systemic racism.

The scope of the plan includes checks and balances across the organization to ensure people are treated with dignity and respect; to examine and evaluate the organization's own biases; to measure, track and review its policies and practices to meet the needs of the community; and finally, to lead change in the communities Froedtert Health serves.

"It is important that health care executives make a statement on diversity

Eradicating inequities and racism will be integral to meeting the needs of all employees, as well as the diverse populations every health system serves.

and inclusion," emphasizes Jacobson. "In some regions, hospitals are the largest employer. They set the standard for other businesses in the marketplace." Froedtert held listening sessions to create its inclusion plan. "We are here to serve everyone in our community," Jacobson says. "Our values of dignity and respect inspire us to create an inclusive and compassionate environment for all people. That sets the framework for providing culturally competent care."

Other health systems are implementing similar initiatives to expand the racial and ethnic composition of their workforces. In the latest *Futurescan* survey, 35 percent of respondents said their hospital or health system already has multiple partnerships and collaborations in place to increase the diversity of its

workforce, and another 33 percent said it is very likely that by 2027, they will have such partnerships.

Conclusion
Over the next five years, C-suite leaders will be focused on finding solutions for maintaining the mental well-being of their staff members, reconfiguring the workforce to reflect changing workflows and the increased use of technology, and eliminating racial bias to ensure all employees can contribute equally to the organization through their diverse talents. "These are complicated issues, and there are no quick solutions," Jacobson says. "But they may well be the most important investments health systems will make in the future success of their organization."

The Acceleration of New Business Models

with Kenneth Kaufman

The post-pandemic era will challenge the most basic assumptions about health care organizations and organizational decision-making, strategy, and thought processes. One of the most critical traditional assumptions is the basic business model and the associated nature of competition, both for hospitals and health systems and for the economy as a whole.

The pandemic reset the U.S. economy, and the reset will reverberate well beyond the end of the pandemic. Every hospital and health system is being challenged to understand how this economic restart is creating competitive stressors and how organizations need to react.

The Current Health Care Landscape

The most pervasive economic reset is the accelerated dominance of the technology sector. "We were already in the midst of a revolution that is fundamentally changing the way we live, work, and relate to one another," says Kenneth Kaufman, managing director and chair of health care consulting firm Kaufman Hall. "This revolution is characterized by high-speed mobile internet, artificial intelligence, automation, big data analytics, and cloud-based technology. These evolving innovations have been delivering substantial improvements in business quality, business speed, and organizational efficiency. They also have led to unforeseen

products and services, as well as radical changes in consumer behavior."

Then the pandemic struck. Verticals with a face-to-face orientation—including bricks-and-mortar retail, restaurants, hospitality, sports, and live entertainment—were decimated by COVID-19. At the same time, big tech never performed better than it did in the first several months of the pandemic. Apple, Amazon, Google and Facebook now account for almost 20 percent of the S&P 500 market cap. Apple, which went public in 1980, took 38 years to reach a $1 trillion market cap. Yet, only two years later, Apple hovered around a $2 trillion market cap (Nicas 2020). In the first two months of the pandemic,

e-commerce market penetration rose 67 percent (Galloway 2020).

"Amazon's growth through the pandemic was breathtaking," says Kaufman. During the second quarter of 2020 and the first wave of the pandemic, Amazon's year-over-year revenue increased 40 percent and its profitability reached more than $5 billion. As the pandemic continued, so did Amazon's revenue growth, increasing 37 percent in the third quarter of 2020. By the end of the third quarter, Amazon's profitability reached more than $6 billion (Amazon Investor Relations 2020).

The reason for big tech's accelerating dominance is its mastery of virtual commerce during a time when face-to-face

About the Subject Matter Expert

Kenneth Kaufman is managing director and chair of health care consulting firm Kaufman Hall, which he cofounded in 1985. For more than 40 years, Kaufman has been one of the leading thinkers on the future of health care. He is the author of seven books and hundreds of articles, and he has delivered more than 400 speeches, most recently focusing on health care disruption. In 2019, he received the Richard L. Clarke Board of Directors Award from the Healthcare Financial Management Association for lifetime contribution to health care.

FUTURESCAN SURVEY RESULTS
Strategy

Health care executives from across the nation were asked how likely it is that the following will happen in their hospital or health system by 2027.

By 2027, our hospital or health system will have increased its investment in digital health care services by at least 30 percent (e.g., digital care in the home, connected and cognitive devices, or artificial intelligence for enhanced diagnosis).

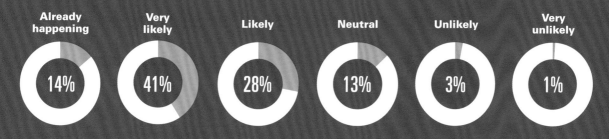

Already happening	Very likely	Likely	Neutral	Unlikely	Very unlikely
14%	41%	28%	13%	3%	1%

By 2027, one or more technology companies will have developed a successful digital platform for managing health care across the continuum.

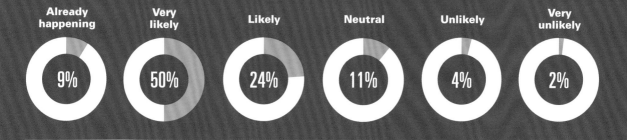

Already happening	Very likely	Likely	Neutral	Unlikely	Very unlikely
9%	50%	24%	11%	4%	2%

commerce was forcibly constricted. However, this phenomenon is not limited to a moment in time caused by a pandemic. Kaufman puts it this way: "The more big tech is winning, the more the nature of competition changes—and that change is likely to be permanent."

In this case, the basis of competition is the ability to provide as many goods and services as possible through virtual connectivity. The winners are the companies that bring the biggest selection, the best experience, and the most digital creativity to the market. And those companies increasingly are consumer centered rather than hospital centered (exhibit 1).

For health care organizations, the critical question is to what extent the business model and nature of competition in health care will be based more on technology and less on face-to-face care delivery. The answer to this question can be divided into two key challenges:

1. The approach to telehealth and digital health care capabilities and delivery.
2. How services are organized and presented to consumers.

Key Challenge 1: Telehealth and Digital Health Care

Before the pandemic, telehealth and digital health care were—despite years of study, testing and promulgation—still in a formative stage. In 2019, only 20 percent of organizations had widely available video visits (Crnkovich et al. 2019).

Then came COVID-19 and, with it, a 154 percent increase in the use of telehealth at the peak of the pandemic's first wave. Many organizations reported accelerating their telehealth plans by years to accommodate the demand from

Exhibit 1

The Consumer Centricity Spectrum

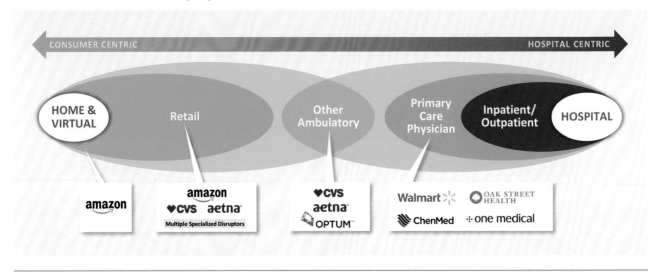

patients unable to see providers in person. Although demand for virtual care has since retreated to a certain extent, many factors argue for the durability of virtual care as a core delivery modality, including virtual care's potential to reduce the unsustainably high total cost of care and patients' positive response to the digital care experience. However, Kaufman says, "Telehealth will be a failure if it goes no further than today's video visits and other routine features."

Siddhartha Mukherjee, MD, DPhil, Pulitzer Prize–winning author, renowned virologist and cancer researcher, made this point forcefully in a presentation during the pandemic (Mukherjee 2020). Too often, he noted, video visits are isolated encounters rather than part of a care plan with measurable goals and steps. Worse still are video visits that conclude simply by scheduling an in-person visit, essentially making the health system bear the cost of two visits instead of one. But the true failure, Mukherjee warned, would be if telehealth does not take advantage of the clinical and cost breakthroughs made possible by increasingly advanced technology leading to a fully integrated digital health platform.

The responsibility of health care providers now is to keep the momentum of telehealth going. That means continuing to promote telehealth to consumers and clinicians. It means improving the execution and efficiency of current practices. It means advocating for fair payment for telehealth services. But most of all, it means developing, investing in and promulgating sophisticated new digital technology that can bring about major advances in outcomes, convenience and affordability.

Implications for Health Care Leaders

Assuming a continued strong demand for virtual care, hospitals and health systems need to think of competition broadly in two new ways:

1. **The extent to which tech companies will continue to encroach on the space of traditional providers.** Amazon, Apple, Google and others have been testing the health care waters for years, and Amazon in particular has recently taken decisive steps in its new integrated virtual, clinic and at-home/at-work health care offerings for employees. Hospitals need to decide whether to partner with or compete against tech companies in digital health care.

2. **How to improve digital offerings as the basis of market competition shifts to greater digital sophistication.** This very expensive proposition requires not only high-end technology but also high-end talent. Only the largest of health systems have the cash flow and capital to support truly transformative digital care strategies.

The results of this year's *Futurescan* survey suggest that hospital and health system executives are taking very seriously the imperative to advance their digital health care strategy. Almost 70 percent of respondents thought it likely or very likely that their hospital or health system will have increased its investment in digital health care services (e.g., digital care in the home, connected and cognitive devices, artificial intelligence for enhanced diagnosis) by at least 30 percent within the next five years. Another 14 percent reported that their organization is already making this kind of investment.

Key Challenge 2: Organization and Presentation of Services

In addition to providing a virtual platform for accessing products and services, companies driving the post-pandemic economy tend to organize their offerings not as one-time transactions but as subscriptions. "Of course, the mother of all subscription offerings in the modern economy is Amazon Prime," says Kaufman.

In this context, the subscription business model means offering a highly valued bundle of products and services at a highly desirable price. This model has many prized features, including revenue reliability, durability and consumer loyalty. The model also has a high barrier to entry. Companies face a steep climb in developing the kinds of products and services that consumers will find unique, essential and in sufficient quantity to warrant a subscription. And even once a sound number of subscribers is achieved, the benefits need to continue growing to keep those subscribers.

The subscription model is so desirable on Wall Street and in the executive suite that even Apple, the most successful brand in history, is moving into subscription bundles as a way of diversifying its revenue.

As new entrants continue to encroach on the health care space, they will apply the principles of the subscription business model to how they organize and deliver services. They will connect consumers to health care services in ways that are so convenient we cannot yet imagine them. And they will use the subscription model to achieve a loyal customer base and a sturdy cash flow.

Scott Galloway, a New York University professor and well-respected analyst of big tech business trends, suggests that Amazon could develop "the most robust, liquid remote healthcare platform on the planet" (Galloway 2020). This platform, which Galloway suggests might be called Prime Health, would be a subscription product fully integrated into the Amazon retail platform that allows "members to get to just the right physician, right now, at lower cost."

The majority of respondents to this year's *Futurescan* survey agree that a big tech company is likely to develop a broad health care platform. Almost three-quarters of executives consider it likely or very likely that by 2027, one or more tech companies will have developed a successful digital platform for managing health care across the continuum of care.

Implications for Health Care Leaders

Just as the pandemic advanced the success of companies like Amazon, the post-pandemic era is likely to accelerate their entrance into health care, especially with the increasing use of remote and virtual options. Amazon is already approaching both large employers and major insurers to expand its Amazon Care solution, which combines virtual and in-person care.

Kaufman points out that "legacy health care organizations have some advantages in their competitive position relative to a company such as Amazon." The most important, according to Kaufman, is that many community members and patient populations are still strongly attached to their traditional hospitals and health systems. "But how long will that attachment last, and how should health care organizations capitalize on it in the meantime?" Kaufman asks. Consumer centeredness is a new basis for competition. Speed to market and achieving sophisticated capabilities are necessary for success. How can they be achieved?

- **Focus on the bundle.** Provider organizations should ask themselves which services would be viewed as highly desirable by a high volume of consumers. One possibility is a hospital-at-home for lower-acuity inpatients, where diagnostic, testing, therapy and other services are provided in the home. Other possible offerings include lower-cost alternatives to hospital-based services (e.g., imaging, ambulatory surgery, other procedural services) as well as the screenings, tests, vaccinations and smoking cessation, weight loss, and yoga programs that constitute so much of a clinic's daily traffic. Other options include in-office services, shorter wait times, direct communication with providers and high-quality video visits.

- **Assess the economics of the bundle.** This extremely sophisticated analysis requires an understanding of fixed and variable costs, potential demand, potential downstream revenue, clinician payment and consumer price sensitivity, among other factors.

- **Develop a digital platform to execute the services.** Health care executives could develop or collaborate on a simple digital system for patients to navigate during their

COVID-19 has catalyzed a major shift in economic and competitive dynamics.

well as of its aggressive culture. Amazon is already in health care. It is lining up assets such as pharmacy fulfillment, data analytics, and on-demand primary care. Amazon can and will continue its encroachment into health care—not all of health care, but the areas it views as profitable. We can expect that Amazon's health care profitability will come at the expense of hospitals' and health systems' performance.

COVID-19 has catalyzed a major shift in economic and competitive dynamics. Few organizations of any kind will find their pre-pandemic strategies to be unaffected. Hospital and health system executives need to carefully and thoroughly assess their organization's capabilities, competitive environment and path forward in a highly disrupted world.

What is needed is not just a review of competitive strategy. Rather, says Kaufman, "Competitive strategy must be informed by a new thought process shaped to confront an economic and competitive environment that, accelerated by the pandemic, is in the process of changing forever."

health care journey. Patients will migrate to the easiest health care solution available.

Conclusion

Once upon a time, Amazon was a customer of FedEx—a really good customer. However, as Amazon Prime increased the quantity, cost and competitive differentiation of Amazon's shipping, Amazon took a different tack. Rather than depend on a vendor—even one like FedEx, credited with revolutionizing the speed and efficiency of shipping—Amazon decided to get into the shipping business. Now, by any measure, Amazon is a more successful shipping company than FedEx.

This is the power of Amazon's capacity for capital and innovation, as

References

Amazon Investor Relations. 2020. "Quarterly Results." Accessed August 26, 2021. https://ir.aboutamazon.com/quarterly-results/default.aspx.

Crnkovich, P., D. Clarin, G. Kingdom, and R. Duffin. 2019. *2019 State of Consumerism in Healthcare: The Bar Is Rising*. Chicago: Kaufman Hall & Associates.

Galloway, S. 2020. *Post Corona: From Crisis to Opportunity*. New York: Portfolio/Penguin.

Mukherjee, S. 2020. "What the Coronavirus Crisis Reveals About American Medicine." Presentation at Kaufman Hall Healthcare Leadership Conference, October 15.

Nicas, J. 2020. "Apple Reaches $2 Trillion, Punctuating Big Tech's Grip." *New York Times*. Published August 19. www.nytimes.com/2020/08/19/technology/apple-2-trillion.html.

Health Care Organizations' Role in Social Justice and Health Equity

with Juana S. Slade

By all accounts, 2020 was a pivotal year that sparked a national reexamination of social injustice, racial bias and health inequities. The COVID-19 pandemic was especially devastating in communities of color, affecting Blacks and Hispanics in much greater numbers than whites. The death of George Floyd and the protests it generated across the country proved to be an equally significant event underscoring the need for change.

In health care, discussions since 2020 have focused not only on racial and ethnic differences in access and outcomes but also on discrimination in the workplace and bias in personnel practices. Health care leaders began to recognize that employees of color bring unique experiences from their communities to the workplace.

Juana S. Slade, chief diversity officer and director of language services at AnMed Health in South Carolina, has been leading the efforts to foster inclusion and diversity at her organization for more than 20 years. Here, she shares learnings not only from her work in that role but also as a founding member of the American Leadership Council of the American Hospital Association's Institute for Diversity and Health Equity.

Key Challenges Facing the Health Care Field

"Although the pursuit of equitable care has a lengthy history, 2020 was the perfect storm that made meaningful discussion about diversity a top priority in many board rooms around the country," Slade states. "The COVID-19 pandemic simply held up a mirror to the inequities that had existed for far too long."

Slade underscores some of the key challenges facing health care leaders in addressing diversity, racial bias and inclusion.

Health inequities. Across the country, Hispanic and African American communities were hit especially hard by COVID-19. Latinx persons have been four times as likely to be hospitalized and twice as likely to die from COVID-19 as non-Hispanic white people. Blacks have been hospitalized three times as often and been twice as likely to die as Caucasians (Rubin-Miller et al. 2020). The toll, however, varies greatly by community. "In South Carolina, Blacks make up 27 percent of the population but account for 41 percent

About the Subject Matter Expert

Juana S. Slade is chief diversity officer and director of language services at AnMed Health, a comprehensive not-for-profit health system serving eight counties in Upstate South Carolina and Northeast Georgia. AnMed Health was one of the first health systems in South Carolina to dedicate full-time resources to strategic diversity management. Its pioneering approach to cultural and linguistic competence has been recognized by the U.S. Department of Health and Human Services' Office for Civil Rights, the Robert Wood Johnson Foundation, the South Carolina Education Television Network and the American Hospital Association. Slade is a member of the board of the South Carolina Hospital Association and chair of the Alliance for a Healthier South Carolina.

FUTURESCAN SURVEY RESULTS
Health Equity

Health care executives from across the nation were asked how likely it is that the following will happen in their hospital or health system by 2027.

By 2027, the ethnic/racial disparities in maternal/child mortality rates at childbirth in our community will be eliminated.

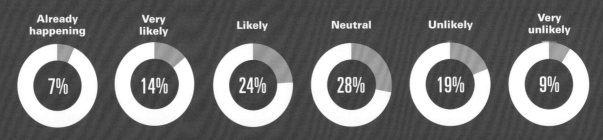

Already happening	Very likely	Likely	Neutral	Unlikely	Very unlikely
7%	14%	24%	28%	19%	9%

By 2027, every patient intake at our hospital or health system will include social determinants of health needs.

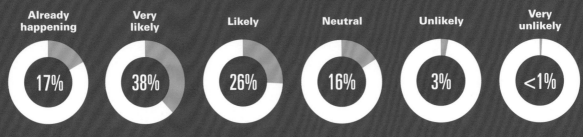

Already happening	Very likely	Likely	Neutral	Unlikely	Very unlikely
17%	38%	26%	16%	3%	<1%

Note: Percentages may not sum exactly to 100 percent because of rounding.

of confirmed COVID-19 cases and 56 percent of deaths from the coronavirus," says Slade.

Health outcome disparities are not isolated to COVID-19 cases. An American College of Physicians study found that Blacks, American Indians and Native Alaskans received poorer care on 40 percent of quality measures compared to whites, while Hispanics fared 35 percent worse and Asian Americans 27 percent worse (Serchen et al. 2021).

Social determinants of health. Residents in communities of color are more likely to work in lower-wage positions and be affected by a lack of safe or stable housing, reliable transportation, nutritious food and access to medical care. All of these social determinants play a role in health outcomes (exhibit 1).

Hospital leaders should be aware of the local social determinants of health (SDOHs) in their community that adversely affect patients' attempts to engage in their own health care because, over time, these SDOHs impact their organization's bottom line. Slade cites the example of one patient who missed three follow-up appointments after discharge. "Although she seemed to be noncompliant, we learned during a follow-up call that she had transportation issues," Slade explains. "To improve care and their own

organization's health, hospital leaders need to be willing to make some infrastructure investments so that they achieve better outcomes." The benefits go beyond creating a more just and inclusive society, Slate notes. "I suggest that C-suite leaders look at their organization's readmission rates stratified by race, ethnicity, income level and zip code to identify any trends that can be used to improve care. From a financial perspective, this exercise is really a strategic initiative on risk mitigation and cost containment."

The latest *Futurescan* survey suggests that screening for SDOH needs during patient intake is far from universal—only 17 percent of respondents said that

Exhibit 1

Social Determinants of Health

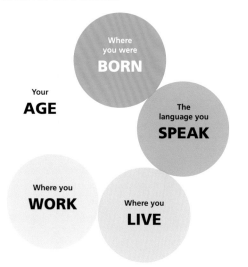

their organization regularly follows this practice. However, 64 percent said it is likely or very likely that patient intake will include such screenings by 2027.

Diversity. Slade maintains that leaders and providers in hospitals and health systems should be racially, ethnically and culturally representative of the communities they serve. This may have implications on whom hospitals recruit and how they ensure they have the right team taking care of patients. "Health care executives also need to consider how they onboard new staff members and how they develop that talent," Slade adds. "Being recruited and being present does not mean you are necessarily engaged in the organization."

Cultural competence. Cultural competence is the ability of providers to effectively deliver health care services that meet the social, cultural and linguistic needs of patients. Clinicians may have biases when interacting with patients and not even be aware of them. "Cultural competence means being able to engage with patients to deliver the best care possible, regardless of whether the provider looks like them, believes as they do or speaks their language," Slade says.

Action Steps for Health Care Leaders

At AnMed, Slade has demonstrated that a health system can make great strides in addressing racial bias and health inequities. She recommends the following strategies.

Develop a diverse organization. Health care leaders should start with the demographics of their community so that they are familiar with the populations and ethnicities in their service area. Recruiting and hiring people from within their community will help both the organization and local residents. Slade suggests that hospitals also conduct an assessment to find out how much they know about themselves, such as how diverse and inclusive they are and whether policies, procedures and cultural norms are executed appropriately. In some cases, new or innovative recruiting strategies

may be required to reach candidates from different cultures or ethnicities.

One such strategy is the Medical Experience (MedEx) Academy, the only program of its kind in the country aimed at attracting high school and undergraduate students from diverse cultural and socioeconomic backgrounds to careers across the broad spectrum of health care professions. MedEx Academy is a collaboration between Prisma Health (South Carolina's largest private, not-for-profit health system) and notable academic institutions such as Clemson University, Furman University and the University of South Carolina. Through a four-tiered process, students are immersed in academic programs, internships, shadowing opportunities and health care exploration designed to help them develop an interest in a health care discipline and commit to a more formal course of study to become a clinician. In 2021, a fifth tier was added to the program to help address students' needs in undergraduate academic performance and success. MedEx Academy has partnered with Harvard Medical School to provide students with an online course that helps them create a more real-world experience with the information they are learning in the classroom.

"The physician shortage in South Carolina places our state forty-third in the nation in terms of primary care physicians per 100,000 residents," says Al Squire, MedEx's executive director. "We also need more nurses, pharmacists and paramedics. It is critical that we build a pipeline to educate our future health care workforce." During its 10 years of operation, MedEx Academy has offered summer experiences to more than 900 students from over 48 high schools in

2020 was the perfect storm that made meaningful discussion about diversity a top priority in many board rooms around the country.

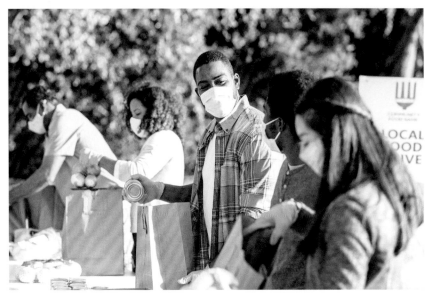

the region and 48 colleges and universities across the country.

Slade advises that recruiters also look internally to identify "untapped gems" in the workforce. "Finding individuals with potential and investing in them through education and training will not only help them advance their careers but also lift their communities and strengthen their connection to the health system," she says.

Foster cultural competence. Medical schools now recognize that cultural competence is an integral part of physician training. Some health systems are beginning to offer cultural competence education as well. Slade suggests that hospital human resources departments seek out external partners who can provide training on working with ethnic and cultural minorities.

At AnMed Health, the Nursing Diversity Advisory Council (NDAC) was created as a way to operationalize language services within the infrastructure of overall nursing practice. It

began with a team of diversity nurse champions who provided feedback on the support they needed to deliver culturally competent care at the bedside. The council meets quarterly and serves as a clinical resource to the diversity and language services department. Its mission is to enable registered nurses at AnMed Health to deliver care that is congruent with cultural diversity and inclusion principles and to promote a nursing environment that does not discriminate based on age, race, ethnicity, religion, culture, language, sexual orientation, or gender identity or expression.

"AnMed provides on-site medical translation services in nine languages, and digital and virtual translation in 200 languages," Slade states. Together with NDAC members, Slade also coordinates training on cultural differences in health beliefs, practices and communication patterns among diverse consumers, families, groups, communities and populations. In the latest nursing satisfaction survey that Slade's department

conducted, more than two-thirds of nurses said they felt the language or diversity issues they encountered were resolved successfully.

Henry Ford Health System in Detroit, Michigan, also has devoted considerable resources to confronting unconscious bias and attaining health equity and cultural competence. Half of the system's senior leaders are women, and 43 percent are persons of color. To reduce disparities and improve outcomes in maternal and infant health, diabetes management and other areas, staff members collect racial, ethnicity and language preference information for more than 90 percent of the health system's patients. As a result, the organization's outcomes show no significant differences between English-proficient patients and limited-English-proficient populations in mortality, readmission or length of stay.

Influence and invest. According to Slade, health system leaders would do well to recognize the power of their influence in their community. AnMed Health's CEO, William A. Kenley, FACHE, underscores that point. "To reduce health disparities, hospital leaders need to explore and address social determinants within the broader community and how they impact overall population health," he says. "Achieving better medical outcomes will require a strategic investment of time and resources, and health systems should determine the most effective way to have an impact on the community and make those investments worthwhile. Fostering inclusion and addressing disparities require that executives embrace authenticity, integrity, transparency and balance."

Finding and collaborating with partners who are already focused on addressing SDOHs can accelerate change for the better within the marketplace. However, Kenley acknowledges that substantive change requires a sustained effort. "What we invest in this year may take one or two years to yield positive results—maybe even longer," he notes. "To measure progress, it is important to set benchmarks and collect metrics such

By making diversity, inclusion and social equity a priority, we can collectively address the health disparities that have persisted in marginalized racial and ethnic minority communities for far too long.

as clinical outcomes stratified by race and ethnicity."

Key Takeaways

Slade and Kenley agree that health care leaders should consider the following when striving to make advances in diversity, inclusion and health equity:

- **Identify key trends.** Analyzing emergency room utilization data can help determine patients' most prevalent health conditions. In addition, the results of any community needs assessments conducted by government agencies, not-for-profits or health systems can focus efforts at addressing health disparities.
- **Reflect the community served.** Ideally, health care leaders, boards of directors, providers and employees would be representative of the community they serve.
- **Eliminate racial bias in hiring and promotions.** Hospitals should conduct an assessment to determine how prevalent fair and inclusive hiring practices, policies and procedures are in the day-to-day work environment.
- **Develop cultural competence.** "The ideal state of health care would be delivering cultural competence at the bedside, in the medical practice, in the ambulatory care center—wherever health services are provided in the community," Slade notes. "A culturally competent health care system can help improve

health outcomes and quality of care, and contribute significantly to the elimination of racial and ethnic health disparities."

- **Find and cultivate partnerships.** Despite having considerable resources, health systems cannot effect change on their own. They should connect with other organizations that are addressing community needs.
- **Influence and invest.** As large employers, hospitals and health systems often have great influence on decision makers at the local, state and national levels. Health care leaders can leverage this advantage in determining the best investments in initiatives that promote social justice and health equity. If housing, food insecurity

or transportation are local issues, they can leverage relationships with local or state government agencies to influence and effect change that can have direct health care implications.

Conclusion

Investments in addressing health inequities will not reduce expenses or improve outcomes immediately, but they will eventually. In the meantime, health systems have a responsibility to care for all residents in their community. "By making diversity, inclusion and social equity a priority, we can collectively address the health disparities that have persisted in marginalized racial and ethnic minority communities for far too long," Slade says.

References

Rubin-Miller, L., C. Alban, S. Artiga and S. Sullivan. 2020. "COVID-19 Racial Disparities in Testing, Infection, Hospitalization, and Death: Analysis of Epic Patient Data." Kaiser Family Foundation. Published September 16. www.kff.org/coronavirus-covid-19/issue-brief/covid-19-racial-disparities-testing-infection-hospitalization-death-analysis-epic-patient-data/.

Serchen, J., R. Doherty, G. Hewett-Abbott, O. Atiq and D. Hilden. 2021. *Understanding and Addressing Disparities and Discrimination Affecting the Health and Health Care of Persons and Populations at Highest Risk.* American College of Physicians. Accessed July 11. www.acponline.org/acp_policy/policies/understanding_discrimination_affecting_health_and_health_care_persons_populations_highest_risk_2021.pdf.

The Future of Provider Reimbursement

with David Blumenthal, MD, HFACHE

When the Affordable Care Act (ACA) became law in 2010, it ushered in many changes in the way providers are reimbursed. Although increases in Medicare expenditures over the past 10 years have been 20 percent lower than projected by Medicare's board of trustees, there is little conclusive evidence that the ACA's goals of lowering costs and improving quality were met (Blumenthal and Abrams 2020).

As the nation continues to struggle with the economic effects of COVID-19, hospitals and health systems likewise are dealing with the financial fallout of significantly diminished revenues during the pandemic's many months. What is the likely reimbursement outlook of government payers and commercial insurers over the next five years? What strategies can help mitigate decreases in reimbursement and better position providers to weather fluctuations in revenue? David Blumenthal, MD, HFACHE, president of The Commonwealth Fund—a private U.S. foundation established to promote better access, improved quality, and greater efficiency in health care—shares his thoughts on the current health care and legislative landscapes.

The Health Care Environment

The United States spends nearly twice as much per capita on health care as any

other developed country with a similar median gross domestic product (Kurani and Cox 2020). In 2018, the cost per person was $10,637 in the United States versus an average of $5,527 in countries such as Austria, Belgium, Canada, France, Germany, the Netherlands, Sweden, Switzerland, and the United Kingdom (exhibit 1). The majority of the U.S. expense—$6,624 per capita—was for inpatient and outpatient care and consisted primarily of payments to hospitals, clinics, primary care physicians and specialists. Abroad, such payments totaled, on average, only $2,718 per capita.

Despite an 8.6 percent decline in overall health care expenditures in the

second quarter of 2020 as many patients delayed or canceled elective procedures during the pandemic (Kamal et al. 2020), economists at the Centers for Medicare & Medicaid Services (CMS) predict that health care expenditures will grow, on average, 5.4 percent annually to reach $6.2 trillion by 2028 (CMS 2020).

With the election of Joseph Biden, efforts are being made to expand Medicaid and reverse policies of the previous administration that made exchange health plans less affordable, less comprehensive in coverage and more difficult to enroll in. Other administrative actions extended the enrollment period for

About the Subject Matter Expert

David Blumenthal, MD, HFACHE, is president of The Commonwealth Fund. Previously, he served as chief health information and innovation officer at Partners Health System and was the Samuel O. Thier Professor of Medicine and Professor of Health Care Policy at Massachusetts General Hospital / Harvard Medical School. From 2009 to 2011, Blumenthal was the National Coordinator for Health Information Technology under President Barack Obama. As a renowned health services researcher and national authority on health information technology adoption, he has authored more than 300 scholarly publications, including seminal studies on the adoption and use of health information technology in the United States.

FUTURESCAN SURVEY RESULTS
Finance

Health care executives from across the nation were asked how likely it is that the following will happen in their hospital or health system by 2027.

By 2027, our hospital or health system will merge with, acquire, or be acquired by another hospital or health system.

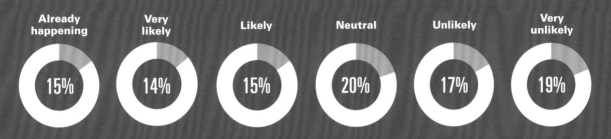

Already happening	Very likely	Likely	Neutral	Unlikely	Very unlikely
15%	14%	15%	20%	17%	19%

By 2027, the proportion of our revenues that will be associated with value-based payments that include downside risk will be at least 30 percent of our total revenues.

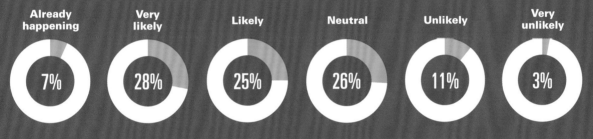

Already happening	Very likely	Likely	Neutral	Unlikely	Very unlikely
7%	28%	25%	26%	11%	3%

the federal marketplace and provided funding for a navigator program to help people sign up for coverage. According to the most recent data from the U.S. Department of Health and Human Services, 2 million additional individuals have enrolled in marketplace plans since the Biden administration opened a special enrollment period in February 2020 (CMS 2021).

With the Supreme Court's decision in June 2021 to let the ACA stand in its current form, additional challenges to dismantle the legislation are unlikely. Instead, stakeholders can expect continued efforts by the Biden administration to make the health insurance marketplace more accessible and the Medicaid program more available to eligible Americans.

Implications for Health Care Leaders

As the single largest payer for health care in this country, the federal government has long set the policies that define how services are reimbursed in both the public and private sectors. "CMS initiated diagnosis-related groups to reduce costs in the 1980s," says Blumenthal. "Despite the subsequent introduction of managed care and Medicare Advantage plans, value-based reimbursement, and bundled payments, the majority of providers are still paid via the fee-for-service model." Blumenthal explains the changes that may be on the horizon from government payers and how commercial insurers will react.

Government payers. The passage in 2021 of the American Rescue Plan Act (ARPA), a $1.9 trillion economic relief package, introduced a number of measures intended to address the economic disruption caused by COVID-19 and to extend health care coverage to uninsured Americans. "I believe we will see CMS place a greater emphasis on enrollment in accountable care organizations and prospective payment for primary care,"

Exhibit 1

Health Care Spending per Capita, 2018

■ Inpatient and outpatient ■ Prescription drugs and medical goods ■ Administrative
■ Long-term ■ Preventive ■ Other

United States (Total: $10,637 per capita)

$6,624			$1,397	$937	$516	$854

Comparable country average (Total: $5,527 per capita)

$2,718	$884	$1,111		

Source: Kurani and Cox (2020).

Blumenthal says. "Increased enrollment in Medicare Advantage plans is likely, as are adjustments in payment rates if Medicare Advantage plans fail to enhance value."

Blumenthal does not expect reductions in fee-for-service reimbursement until COVID-19 is under control and health care utilization returns to near-normal levels. He believes the Biden administration will accelerate work on new value-based and prospective payment models. In this regard, providers and insurers should expect government initiatives to include measures of equity in definitions of value under value-based payment formulas. No administration in recent history has so strongly committed to addressing long-standing disparities in health care among persons of color in the United States, and CMS will likely experiment with a variety of ways to motivate private sector payers to work on addressing these inequities.

"One of the most significant developments impacting the financial outlook for health care reimbursement is the federal deficit, which greatly increased with the passage of the ARPA," notes Blumenthal. "Before the ARPA, Medicare was predicted to be insolvent by 2026. The expanded deficit may impede efforts to extend the time to insolvency and increase pressure to identify ways to contain Medicare and Medicaid spending, unless the federal government finds ways to increase revenues."

Blumenthal adds that the deficit will likely lead to more calls for reducing overall public sector spending on social programs, although the Biden administration seems intent on enacting its comprehensive social spending agenda. Possible inflation and associated interest rate increases are also important factors. "If interest rates rise, they could make the government's debt more difficult to service and put additional pressure on both entitlement and discretionary federal spending," Blumenthal says.

Another factor accelerating cost pressures is the rapid rate at which baby boomers are aging into Medicare (exhibit 2). A large influx of new beneficiaries could result in greater expenditures than anticipated, although younger beneficiaries fortunately tend to incur lower per capita costs than older ones.

Still another area of ongoing interest among government payers and public policy decision makers is continuing pressure on providers to exchange health data not only with other private entities but also with public health authorities. New regulations implementing the 21st Century Cures Act are already well underway and include significant financial penalties for so-called information blocking. What is more, the pandemic has highlighted the tangible human and economic costs of our nation's inability to coordinate care in response to external infectious threats. The ARPA contains substantial funding for modernizing the public health information infrastructure. Providers should expect to be drawn into discussions with local health authorities about the best way to ensure the interoperability of a modernized public health data infrastructure with private data systems.

Commercial insurers. Blumenthal does not believe a single payer system

> Providers should expect government initiatives to include measures of equity in definitions of value under value-based payment formulas.

Exhibit 2

Projected Medicare Spending

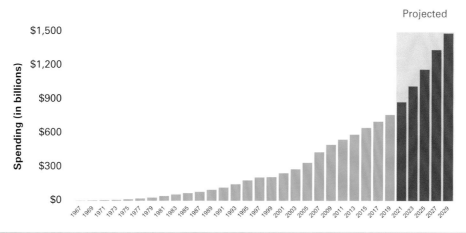

Source: Commonwealth Fund (2020).

is on the horizon, so commercial and private payers will be part of the reimbursement milieu for the foreseeable future. However, the pandemic may have lingering effects on commercial insurers. "Provider consolidations may gather momentum in the wake of the pandemic as weak medical practices and financially challenged hospitals look to align with more sustainable institutions," Blumenthal says. "That could lead to upward pressure on pricing and thus insurance rates."

Commercial insurers may employ other strategies to enhance profitability. To contain costs and attain more efficient, higher-quality care, some payers may expand their business portfolios into care delivery. UnitedHealth Group's OptumHealth division has been acquiring physician practices at a rapid rate. The largest recent acquisition was Atrius Health, a Boston-based not-for-profit with more than 700 physicians. Its acquisition strategy has helped make OptumHealth a lucrative division of UnitedHealth, contributing $3.4 billion in operating profits in 2020 (Tozzi 2021). However, Blumenthal cautions, "Managing providers, and especially physicians, may prove challenging for payers, and it would not be surprising to see some of these acquisitions spun off over time."

This year's *Futurescan* survey shows health system executives almost evenly divided on the likelihood that their organization will be involved in a merger or acquisition over the next five years. This response could be a reflection of the uncertain environment at the time of the survey and the multiple factors that would need to converge to make such an affiliation a strategic imperative. Certainly, the post-COVID-19 environment is extremely fluid. But if even a quarter of respondents' organizations were to enter into a merger, preexisting trends toward provider consolidation could accelerate.

In another marketplace development, Blumenthal has observed some providers seeking a market advantage by delivering higher-quality care more efficiently. Miami-based ChenMed is a full-risk Medicare Advantage provider for moderate- to low-income seniors and receives a fixed amount per patient for overall health care costs. The

family-owned organization currently operates more than 75 medical centers in 12 states, and the company expects to open 25 more centers by the end of 2021.

ChenMed doctors intentionally care for only one-fifth as many patients as the national primary care physician panel average of 2,300 patients. By serving just 400 to 450 patients, ChenMed's primary care physicians invest substantially more time with patients, both one-on-one in the exam room and in follow-up. ChenMed patients receive highly personalized care with a focus on disease prevention, early diagnosis and reduction in hospital sick days.

ChenMed patients have their primary care doctor's cell phone number and are permitted to call or text anytime. They also enjoy same-day telemedicine or walk-in appointments, complimentary transportation to doctor visits, and on-site specialists and medication dispensing. With 73 percent of its

> The pandemic has highlighted the tangible human and economic costs of our nation's inability to coordinate care in response to external infectious threats.

patient population having five or more comorbidities, ChenMed emphasizes frequent patient interactions to effectively manage chronic conditions.

"Our high-touch approach prevents little problems from becoming big ones," explains Gordon Chen, MD, ChenMed's chief medical officer. "And our being a full-risk Medicare Advantage provider means our doctors do better when we help our patients achieve better health and avoid preventable hospitalizations. Aligned incentives actually help every patient enjoy better health, and that's precisely why we consistently reduce in-patient hospital admissions by 30 to 50 percent, even for our many patients with multiple and major chronic conditions." At the end of 2020, ChenMed and six like-minded provider organizations sent a letter to CMS encouraging the agency to remove current barriers that limit Medicare Advantage competition. Full-risk providers like ChenMed also enjoyed an unexpected financial advantage during the pandemic because their revenues were not tied to the fee-for-service volumes that dropped dramatically in 2020.

According to the results of the *Futurescan* survey, few organizations—just 7 percent—are already engaged in value-based payments to the degree that they comprise at least 30 percent of revenues. However, 53 percent of respondents said this scenario is either likely or very likely to occur in the next

five years, a trend that Blumenthal believes could significantly improve health system performance and patient care.

Blumenthal says that pricing transparency is another factor that may affect provider reimbursement from the commercial sector. "When rates for health care services become widely accessible, they can be used by private insurers to negotiate contracts, and by employers to identify centers of excellence and to direct employees to shoppable services." For example, Walmart refers employees to 17 health system partners for episodes of care, which are funded via prenegotiated bundled payments (Gamble 2021).

Key Takeaways for Health Care Leaders

Blumenthal's role at The Commonwealth Fund is to promote better health care access and improved quality, especially for the elderly and society's most vulnerable. Health care executives may find the following strategies appealing when planning for the next five years.

- **Consolidate and grow.** To protect their organization, some C-suite leaders will find it attractive to acquire or partner with additional health care resources across the continuum to become more dominant and less likely to be excluded from health plan panels. These resources

may include skilled nursing facilities, freestanding rehabilitation centers, hospice and home health agencies, and more.

- **Diversify.** The pandemic was especially detrimental to hospitals and health systems that relied on fee-for-service patient volumes for survival. Those that had entered into value-based contracts received a steady stream of revenue despite the drop in services provided. Health systems that have acquired or started their own insurance companies are able to control pricing and utilization, but a downside risk to this strategy is that other insurers may view the organization as a competitor.

- **Manage transparency.** Blumenthal believes health care leaders will have to grapple with how their pricing compares to that of their competitors and how it affects their strategic planning. Depending on how competitive their marketplace is, they may benefit from lowering their costs or prices to be more competitive. As pricing becomes more transparent, payers and employers may use this information to negotiate more favorable contracts or require patients to use lower-cost providers.

- **Address health inequities.** The COVID-19 pandemic highlighted the degree of health care disparities that exist in this country. Programs to address systemic racism will become very important. Blumenthal says, "I expect that Medicare and Medicaid may move to address health inequities, along with larger community not-for-profits."

Conclusion

Financial incentives are still not properly aligned to drive value-based care, according to Blumenthal. However, external pressures may continue to move health care reimbursement toward prospective payment models, where providers assume the downside risk for health care costs. Health care executives would be wise to position their organization for this eventuality while operating as efficiently as possible in the current environment.

References

Blumenthal, D., and M. Abrams. 2020. "The Affordable Care Act at 10 Years—Payment and Delivery." *New England Journal of Medicine* 382 (11): 1057–64.

Centers for Medicare & Medicaid Services (CMS). 2021. "Health Care Sign Ups Surpass 2 Million During 2021 Special Enrollment Period Ahead of Aug. 15 Deadline." Published July 14. www.cms.gov/newsroom/press-releases/health-care-sign-ups-surpass-2-million-during-2021-special-enrollment-period-ahead-aug-15-deadline.

———. 2020. *National Health Expenditure Fact Sheet.* Modified December 16. www.cms.gov/Research-Statistics-Data-and-Systems/Statistics-Trends-and-Reports/NationalHealthExpendData/NHE-Fact-Sheet.

Commonwealth Fund. 2020. "Medicare Data Hub." Published October. www.commonwealthfund.org/sites/default/files/2020-10/Medicare%20Data%20Hub_October2020.pdf.

Gamble, M. 2021. "The 17 Health Systems to Which Walmart Sends Employees for Care in 2021." *Becker's Hospital Review.* Published June 11. www.beckershospitalreview.com/strategy/the-17-health-systems-to-which-walmart-sends-employees-for-care-in-2021.html.

Kamal, R., D. McDermott, G. Ramirez and C. Cox. 2020. "How Has U.S. Spending on Healthcare Changed over Time?" Peterson-KFF Health System Tracker. Published December 23. www.healthsystemtracker.org/chart-collection/u-s-spending-healthcare-changed-time/.

Kurani, N., and C. Cox. 2020. "What Drives Health Spending in the U.S. Compared to Other Countries." Peterson-KFF Health System Tracker. Published September 25. www.healthsystemtracker.org/brief/what-drives-health-spending-in-the-u-s-compared-to-other-countries/.

Tozzi, J. 2021. "UnitedHealth Chases 10,000 More Doctors for Biggest U.S. Network." *Bloomberg.* Published March 5. www.bloomberg.com/news/articles/2021-03-05/unitedhealth-s-deal-machine-scoops-up-covid-hit-doctor-groups.

Post-COVID Virtual Health Strategies

with Randy D. Oostra, DM, FACHE

During the COVID-19 pandemic, the use of telehealth increased exponentially when the Centers for Medicare & Medicaid Services sanctioned its reimbursement and other payers followed suit. Consumers who were reluctant to visit clinics or hospitals embraced the opportunity to interact with their doctors virtually. Consumers had good experiences overall, with many finding telehealth easier to access and more efficient than traditional office visits.

According to Randy D. Oostra, DM, FACHE, the president and CEO of ProMedica, a not-for-profit health system serving communities in 28 states, telemedicine may be the most prevalent form of virtual health but will soon be far from the only one. He predicts rapid and widespread adoption of a variety of virtual health business models by players both inside and outside legacy health care systems. The opportunities are abundant, and innovation will make them even more patient centered, cost-effective and easy to access.

ProMedica is an early adopter of some of these models. Oostra offers his thoughts on how virtual health will transform care delivery over the next five years and what health system leaders should know if they are considering virtual care delivery options.

The Current Health Care Landscape

The COVID-19 pandemic dramatically altered the way health care is delivered, and not just from a telemedicine perspective. In early 2020, just as the pandemic was beginning to affect hospitals around the country, Medicare granted waivers to 130 organizations to provide hospital-at-home services. Oostra expects to see this model of care implemented more widely in the post-pandemic environment, potentially transforming the delivery of acute care. "Hospital and health system executives may find themselves at a crossroads," he says. "Do they embrace alternative care delivery models by developing them for the future, and if so, how will that impact their current operations and reimbursement under existing payment models?"

Oostra says a lot of innovation and consumer acceptance has happened in a very short period of time. "Patients have become comfortable using virtual care. Employers will want these services for their workers as well, especially if they can be delivered at a lower cost." He adds that baby boomers are now more computer savvy than ever before: "They are joining millennials and Gen Xers in

About the Subject Matter Expert

Randy D. Oostra, DM, FACHE, is the president and CEO of ProMedica, the not-for-profit integrated health and well-being organization headquartered in Toledo, Ohio. He is regarded as one of the nation's top leaders in health care and has been included among *Modern Healthcare*'s 100 Most Influential People in Healthcare and *Becker's Healthcare*'s 100 Great Leaders in Healthcare. Oostra was honored with the Jefferson Award for Public Service and the Ohio Hospital Association's Donald R. Newkirk Award for making a significant lifetime contribution to the health care industry. He is a Fellow of the American College of Healthcare Executives.

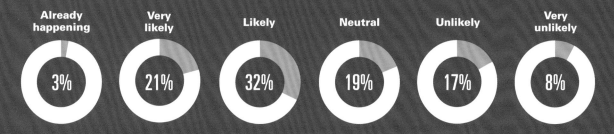
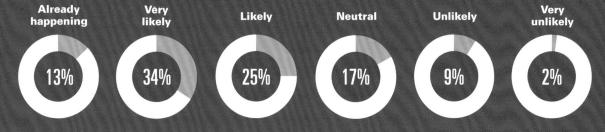
demanding virtual health services. The overarching question is, will telehealth replace traditional visits, or will they improve access?" That question emerged when urgent care centers were first being developed. Many experts initially believed they would decrease patient volumes in emergency rooms. "That didn't happen," Oostra notes. "We found that they actually helped triage patients to the hospital."

The hospital-at-home model is a concept with which Oostra is familiar. ProMedica, which has its own insurance plan, initially began caring in early 2020 for 60 patients who had a chronic obstructive pulmonary disease diagnosis. As the pandemic wore on, ProMedica also began caring for COVID-19 patients in their homes. "The technology exists now for many health care services to be provided in the home," he asserts. "Home care can be more efficient and effective."

A study conducted by a team of researchers at Atrium Health, a North Carolina–based health system with 40 hospitals and more than 1,400 locations across four states, has helped prove the efficacy of the hospital-at-home model. The research concluded that Atrium Health Hospital at Home (AH-HaH) is a safe, patient-centered care delivery model for appropriately selected patients (Chou et al. 2021). Early in the pandemic, Atrium Health set up a virtual hospital to use telemedicine to treat COVID-19 patients who did not require intensive care in their homes. Eligible patients received a home monitoring kit containing a blood pressure monitor, pulse oximeter,

thermometer and detailed instructions for use. Patients received daily assessment calls from a nurse, virtual visits with a provider and daily in-home visits by a community paramedic. AH-HaH helped manage the surge in COVID-19 patients by keeping moderately ill patients out of the hospital and in the comfort of their homes.

The hospital-at-home concept has other advantages, according to Oostra. Because clinicians visit patients in their residence, it allows them to see their living environment. Such visitations can yield important clues to lifestyle factors that may be affecting a patient's health. "One of the most significant benefits of the hospital-at-home model of care is that it can help keep older adults at home longer and living independently," he notes. "It can also keep them in skilled nursing longer and out of the acute care setting. Many homes are now being built with the technological infrastructure to deliver home health services, including robust broadband connectivity."

According to the latest *Futurescan* survey, very few respondents (only 3 percent) reported that the hospital-

at-home treatment model was already happening in their organization. But many see the efficacy of the model: More than half (53 percent) believe it is likely or very likely that at least 50 percent of stable, chronically ill patients with acute medical problems will be treated via hospital-at-home services rather than inpatient care by 2027.

Other virtual health applications that health system leaders may want to explore include:

- Virtual specialty care, such as at-home infusions for cancer patients, dietary and counseling management of high-cost chronic diseases like diabetes, and musculoskeletal care that uses artificial intelligence and video capture to track and accelerate recovery from injuries or surgery.
- Comprehensive suites of aging-related services that assess the needs of individual seniors and provide a single source of products, services, information and education specifically curated to the needs of the aging population.
- The sharing of specialist clinicians via telehealth under formal arrangements with other organizations. Nearly

60 percent of respondents in the *Futurescan* survey agreed that clinician sharing was either likely or very likely over the next five years.

- An expansion of employer health and well-being programs to address the social determinants of health (SDOHs) that affect employee productivity. Issues such as unstable housing, food insecurity and lack of transportation drive higher emergency room visits, greater likelihood of depression and elevated health care expenses for payers and employers.

Implications for Health Care Leaders

Oostra believes the debate over virtual care strategies will be driven in large part by reimbursement. "Are you actively going to cannibalize your current services to give your consumers what they want?" he asks. Given the popularity of virtual health services, Oostra offers some considerations that C-suite executives may want to weigh before deciding where to invest their resources.

Competition. Nontraditional providers have been entering the health care space in a big way. Amazon, Google, CVS and Walmart are reaching directly to consumers to provide primary care and even specialty services via increasingly convenient platforms.

Virtual care presents competitive challenges, as traditional footprints and regional boundaries are expanded and blurred by the digital extension of both traditional health care players and new commercial ventures looking to leverage themselves into these opportunities. And because licensing and regulatory rules governing care provision and providers are all variably mediated by individual state medical boards, additional complexities and costs will be incurred as interstate telehealth workflows continue to expand in scope and volume.

Capital investments. Many health systems have made significant investments in brick-and-mortar buildings. However, virtual care services are largely delivered in homes or out in the community. If this mode of delivery prevails,

---

Telemedicine may be the most prevalent form of virtual health but will soon be far from the only one.

---

whole wings of hospitals may eventually be empty.

Dollars may need to be redirected toward information technology investments. The challenge, according to Oostra, is to rethink the role technology plays outside the hospital setting. What is the potential direct loss of revenue, and can you deliver virtual health services profitably? Is there a way to limit the amount spent on capital investment and divert it to technological infrastructure?

Hospital-based organizations without experience and expertise in the provision of virtual care will be climbing a steep learning curve. "Managing the business model, revenue cycles and even supply chain requires a radically different skill set than traditional, facility-based hospital operations do," Oostra asserts.

Impact on providers. "Telehealth works to varying degrees, depending on the specialty," Oostra notes. With the widespread use of telehealth during the pandemic, many providers were forced to use a platform that was relatively new. "While some clinicians felt it was an option that is here to stay, others said they weren't trained for telehealth and went back to in-person visits," Oostra explains. Fundamental questions arose: What is the impact on physician reimbursement? Can physicians be more productive and efficient through telehealth? Will the widespread use of telehealth or physician extenders jeopardize their income?

Impact on social determinants of health. Telehealth improves access for many populations that traditionally have been limited in their ability to find health care. Not coincidentally, these same communities often struggle with SDOHs such as access to fresh and healthful food, safe and stable housing, and readily available transportation. Addressing these issues through targeted interventions improves health outcomes while reducing utilization.

According to Oostra, employer workforces are also vulnerable to fluctuations in their ability to meet basic needs. ProMedica is piloting a virtual health

screening application called Resourceful that can help employers identify and quantify the issues that affect employee health and productivity the most. "Everyone struggles from time to time," Oostra asserts. "Financial insecurity, unstable housing situations, lack of food and other necessities, and childcare or transportation challenges impact people at surprising rates. When these essential needs go unmet, employers pay through higher health care costs, lost productivity and turnover." According to proprietary data from Front Health, a health system collaborative that ProMedica helped start, employers whose workforce lacks essential needs have 14 percent higher health care costs and a 28 percent higher rate of emergency room utilization. They also incur $2 billion a year in costs related to absenteeism (Asay et al. 2016).

Resourceful closes the gap between workers' needs and better health and well-being by connecting workers confidentially with the assistance they require, including low- or no-cost groceries, behavioral health services, child care and stable housing. ProMedica has launched multiple Resourceful

pilots with its own employees. Of the 600 who engaged with the virtual app, 67 percent cited stress as their primary concern, 48 percent said depression was their greatest issue, and 46 percent were feeling financial strain. Food was the biggest priority for 24 percent of respondents. "We are now convinced that our current wellness offerings have been missing the mark," declares Oostra. "They have not addressed the health and well-being of our employees in a holistic way. We believe that looking beyond the traditional approach to wellness will lead to happier, healthier employees and, ultimately, to better engagement, retention and lower health care costs." Employers who are interested in lowering their health care costs and increasing productivity may find Resourceful an efficient way to meet both goals.

Key Takeaways
As health care transitions to a value-based environment, Oostra believes that virtual health will play a major role in containing costs and improving quality and access. By efficiently delivering care in the low-cost home or community

Virtual health will play a major role in containing costs and improving quality and access.

setting, hospitals and health systems may be able to scale their services into at-risk contracts and share the significant savings with payers. Just as important, patients are ultimately healthier and stay in their own homes, improving their life experience.

According to Oostra, "The challenge for health care leaders exploring virtual health will be keeping pace with the technology and efficiently integrating new workflows into existing care models, while also differentiating the organization and its services to consumers, payers and employers." He offers the following advice for hospital executives:

- **View patients as consumers.** They will continue to have more choices as nontraditional providers introduce new health care access points along the continuum.
- **Reevaluate investments in brick and mortar.** Consumers are embracing the ability to seek medical care at home or outside the four walls of the hospital.

- **Consider how to deliver current services in nontraditional ways.** Use of telehealth platforms and remote patient monitoring to deliver care more efficiently in the low-cost home setting not only improves access and preserves current revenue sources but also creates new revenue growth opportunities.
- **Evaluate the costs.** Up-front expenses to create a virtual health platform and care flows are high, and so are the risks. Hospitals with heavy fixed costs also need to guard against potential cannibalization of margins, planning and strategizing accordingly.
- **Look for collaborators.** Instead of building new virtual health services, Oostra suggests collaborating with an experienced provider that aligns with your organization's vision and purpose. "Businesses that already have well-developed models in this arena can bring geographic reach and patient volumes with only incremental costs," he states. "It

may be more strategic to contract with payers in creative three-way agreements or to enter joint ventures or risk-sharing arrangements with partner organizations in this space. Any of these options can expedite cost-effective growth and expansion in virtual care models."

Conclusion

The next decade of revenue growth in health care will be driven by progressively more sophisticated, patient-centered and home-focused models of care. "Telehealth and virtual care can address a lot of the inefficiency and inequity in care and access," Oostra states. "If we get it right, we can put more affordable and accessible services in people's hands. If the waste in the health care system can be eliminated, the cost savings will pay for these technologies. Telehealth is the perfect platform to gather all the disparate pieces of health care into one comprehensive system."

References

Asay, G.R.B., R. Kakoli, J.E. Lang, R.L. Payne and D. Howard. 2016. "Absenteeism and Employer Costs Associated with Chronic Diseases and Health Risk Factors in the US Workforce." *Preventing Chronic Disease.* Published October 6. http://dx.doi.org/10.5888/pcd13.150503external icon.

Chou, S.-H., A. McWilliams, S. Murphy, K. Sitammagari, T.-L. Liu, C. Hole and M. Kowalkowski. 2021. "Factors Associated with Risk for Care Escalation Among Patients with COVID-19 Receiving Home-Based Hospital Care." *Annals of Internal Medicine* 174 (8): 1188–91.

The Growing Importance of Behavioral Health in the COVID and Post-COVID Landscape

with Harsh K. Trivedi, MD

Behavioral health services have been undervalued and underfunded for many years, making them unprofitable service lines for most health systems. In a recent survey, nearly a quarter of health care chief financial officers said their organizations plan to divest from behavioral health services (Bryant 2021). Over time, the United States has experienced a steep decline in inpatient behavioral health care beds, with a per capita psychiatric bed count that is approximately 70 percent lower than the average in other developed nations (Bastiampillai, Sharfstein and Allison 2016). "Even before the COVID-19 pandemic, suicide rates were at their highest in 30 years, and opioid abuse had reached crisis proportions, along with anxiety and depression," says Harsh K. Trivedi, MD, president and CEO of Sheppard Pratt, the nation's largest private, not-for-profit provider of mental health, substance use, developmental disability, special education and social services. "The pandemic has amplified these trends and exacerbated an already-grim outlook for the provision of mental health services not just in the overall population, but especially in communities of color."

As the country's health care system moves toward value-based care, Trivedi emphasizes that greater investment in behavioral health services is needed. A study of 2017 claims data for 21 million patients found that although individuals with both behavioral health and physical conditions generated the highest health care expenditures overall, 75 percent had total annual behavioral health treatment costs of only $502 or less, even when they were diagnosed or treated by a health care professional for a behavioral illness (Davenport, Gray and Melek 2020). In fact, behavioral health treatment costs amounted to just 4.4 percent of total health care expenditures.

The statistics on access to behavioral health care among persons of color are even more concerning. The treatment gaps for mental illness and depression are significantly greater among Blacks and Hispanics than in the overall U.S. population (exhibit 1). In addition, 89 percent of Blacks and 90 percent of Hispanics report receiving no treatment for substance use disorders. Native Americans are more likely to need treatment for alcohol or illicit drug use than are persons of any other ethnic group; but while 13 percent of Native Americans need substance use treatment, less than 4 percent actually receive it (SAMHSA 2020b). Clearly, more effort needs to be expended to erase racial inequities in access to mental health care.

About the Subject Matter Expert

Harsh K. Trivedi, MD, is the president and CEO of Sheppard Pratt. He is also a clinical professor of psychiatry at the University of Maryland School of Medicine and a nationally renowned expert in health care, hospital systems, care delivery, population health and behavioral health. He currently serves on the American Hospital Association board of trustees, the board of the National Association for Behavioral Healthcare, and the executive committee of the Maryland Hospital Association. He is active in his local community and serves on the board of the Baltimore Community Foundation.

FUTURESCAN SURVEY RESULTS
Behavioral Health

Health care executives from across the nation were asked how likely it is that the following will happen in their hospital or health system by 2027.

By 2027, the number of opioid-related deaths in our community will decrease by 50 percent.

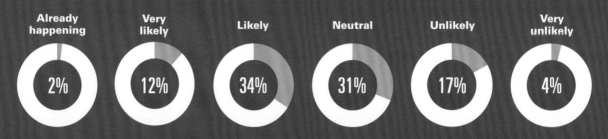

Already happening	Very likely	Likely	Neutral	Unlikely	Very unlikely
2%	12%	34%	31%	17%	4%

By 2027, our hospital or health system will no longer board psychiatric patients in the emergency department because of increased availability of other behavioral health resources.

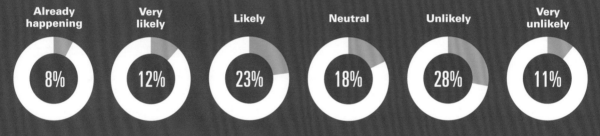

Already happening	Very likely	Likely	Neutral	Unlikely	Very unlikely
8%	12%	23%	18%	28%	11%

Considerable evidence suggests that addressing behavioral health issues in a collaborative care model with primary care yields significantly better outcomes and lowers overall costs. In the first landmark study of its kind, the *Journal of the American Medical Association* published the results of the largest depression treatment trial conducted to date in 2002. Called the IMPACT study (reflecting the name of the model, Improving Mood—Promoting Access to Collaborative Treatment), the *JAMA* article detailed the effectiveness of collaborative care in managing depression in older adults. The research followed more than 1,800 adults divided into two groups: One cohort received the normal course of care in a primary care setting—antidepressant medication and referral to a mental health specialist—while the other cohort was treated using the IMPACT model, in which a care manager and psychiatrist join the primary care provider in developing and administering a course of treatment.

The IMPACT study found that collaborative care improved the effectiveness of depression treatment by more than double in primary care settings while also reducing its cost. One year into the trial, about half of the patients in the collaborative care cohort had at least a 50 percent reduction in depressive symptoms, compared with only 19 percent of patients treated in the traditional primary care model. The study concluded that for every dollar spent on collaborative care, up to six dollars are saved (Unützer et al. 2002).

A more recent study supported the value of collaborative care in treating depression and anxiety. The review examined 79 randomized controlled trials and included more than 24,000 patients worldwide. The researchers concluded that collaborative care resulted in significant improvement in depression and anxiety outcomes, and it increased the number of patients using medication in line with current guidelines (Archer et al. 2012). Those treated with collaborative care were also more satisfied with their treatment.

"With health systems accepting more risk for population health, C-suite executives should consider expanding their behavioral health services or find ways to partner with other organizations to provide these services to patients," Trivedi states. "There is more than ample evidence that investing in behavioral health care substantially impacts medical and surgical spend downstream."

Key Challenges Facing the Health Care Field

The COVID-19 pandemic had a negative impact on an already-tenuous mental health safety net, and hospitals are feeling the effects in several ways. Many inpatient psychiatric units had to be repurposed to provide overflow or COVID-19 beds. There is still uncertainty as to when these beds will be returned to use for behavioral health patients.

As a result, the problem of boarding patients in emergency departments (EDs) has grown. Median ED visit counts between March 15, 2020, and October 10, 2020, for suicide attempts, drug overdoses and opioid overdoses were significantly higher than during the same period in 2019 (Holland, Jones and Vivolo-Kantor 2021). When coupled with the critical shortage of mental health beds, the dramatic increase in mentally distressed patients has increasingly required them to be boarded in hospital EDs, and the wait for a bed can be lengthy. The results of the latest

Futurescan survey indicate that health system leaders vary in their expectation that boarding psychiatric patients in the ED will no longer occur over the next five years. The number of respondents who believe it likely (35 percent) was nearly equal to those who think it unlikely (39 percent), with another 18 percent remaining neutral on the subject. Only 8 percent said that their organizations were no longer holding psychiatric patients in the ED.

Another challenge for health care leaders is the impending shortage of qualified behavioral health professionals. Seventy-seven percent of U.S. counties face a serious shortage of psychiatrists (Merritt Hawkins 2018), and the American Academy of Medical Colleges (AAMC 2015) predicts a deficit of as many as 3,400 psychiatrists by 2032. An additional concern is that more than 60 percent of practicing psychiatrists are over the age of 55 and are thus approaching retirement (AAMC 2015).

A lack of diversity among mental health care providers is also an issue (American Psychiatric Association 2017).

Because of the weakened U.S. economy, many families are suffering financially and either lack or have lost behavioral health care coverage. Lower-wage workers are more likely to be people of color, who tend to work in sectors hit hardest by the economic downturn. When dollars are scarce and are needed to pay for food, housing and transportation, addressing behavioral health conditions becomes a low priority.

Strategies for Health Care Leaders

"There is no magic bullet to fix the behavioral health care system," Trivedi notes. "However, mental health care holds greater promise for keeping people well and lowering costs than any other health care segment." Although every community is different, an effective mental health ecosystem consists of

Exhibit 1

Percentage of U.S. Population Reporting No Treatment Received

Demographic	Any mental illness	Serious mental illness	Major depressive episode
Blacks	69%	42%	65%
Hispanics	67%	44%	62%
Overall	57%	36%	59%

Source: SAMHSA (2020a).

inpatient units, crisis intervention services, intensive outpatient or partial hospitalization programs, and outpatient care. Trivedi adds that providing support services and managing social determinants of health are important adjuncts to a robust behavioral health care continuum.

Knowing that funding is limited, Trivedi suggests that health care leaders start by reviewing already-completed community health needs assessments that may highlight gaps in mental health services or social determinants of health. "That will help identify potential partners for collaboration on developing or investing in behavioral health services," he points out. "Many agencies have been living and breathing this world for decades."

Other strategies may be gleaned from case studies of successful behavioral health initiatives such as those implemented at WakeMed Health and Hospitals, Sheppard Pratt, and Avera Health.

WakeMed Health and Hospitals. In 2017, North Carolina–based WakeMed Health and Hospitals was being inundated by patients with substance use and behavioral health issues. The system's seven EDs documented more than 40,000 encounters with such patients, and its three hospitals had an average daily census of 150 patients but no psychiatric beds or organized programs to treat them. Many resources for treating these patients already existed in the surrounding area, but they were not properly coordinated. WakeMed's leadership felt an imperative to create an interconnected behavioral health network and a circle of support for patients.

In response, WakeMed launched the Network for Advancing Behavioral Health, which consists of outpatient clinicians who provide psychiatric care, outpatient therapy and evidence-based programs such as medication-assisted treatment. WakeMed Health went on to establish another collaborative, the Connected Community, to help patients access social services agencies that address needs related to housing, food security, transportation and personal safety. A final network called the Behavioral Health Council added access to nearly 1,000 beds across several inpatient behavioral health institutions. Collectively, these three networks form the WakeMed Behavioral Health Network, and more than 30 different partner organizations are actively involved. A key part of the initiative has been the development of a proprietary tiering process, based on severity of illness, that quickly connects patients to the right care.

The linkages that WakeMed has built are having a dramatic effect on patient access in the broader community. The organization has seen an 87 percent decrease in state hospital referrals and an 80 percent decrease in avoidable bed days (time spent waiting at WakeMed for placement at a psychiatric or substance use care provider in the community).

Sheppard Pratt. At the beginning of the COVID-19 pandemic, Maryland-based Sheppard Pratt quickly recognized the heightened need for behavioral health services, and instead of limiting access to providers, the organization created new modes of delivery. The Virtual Crisis Walk-In Clinic was developed as an alternative to hospital EDs and recorded nearly 4,500 visits from early April through December 2020. The virtual clinic helped decrease the volume of psychiatric patients in EDs where COVID-positive patients were being treated. The service uses a secure online platform to conduct urgent psychiatric evaluations and to refer patients to other virtual and in-person care options.

In addition, Sheppard Pratt expanded access to critical services in the community. Staff members were redeployed to conduct home visits across 200 supportive housing locations—delivering over 250,000 meals and providing more than 130,000 diapers to families in need. Access to critical programs was further supported through more than $2 million in funding from the U.S. Department of Veterans Affairs to support Sheppard Pratt's housing assistance program for veterans, which helps individual veterans and their families to secure permanent

Investing in behavioral health care now will pay great dividends in keeping entire populations healthy for the long term.

housing and provides temporary financial assistance with housing or moving expenses. The funding also helped launch Sheppard Pratt's new health navigation services, which connect veterans with physical, mental and substance use treatments that are needed now more than ever.

The organization also responded to the many stressors its own employees were experiencing. Telehealth counseling and therapy groups were offered free of charge to those who wanted them. For employees with children, five day camps staffed by Sheppard Pratt's own school-based employees provided a safe place for kids who could no longer visit a classroom. "We continue to respond and provide innovative solutions to meet the needs of our patients, clients, students and our employees as our country moves toward recovery from the pandemic," notes Trivedi. "We recognize that we are facing a worsening mental health crisis, and the need for mental health services has never been greater."

Avera Health. As difficult as it is to find mental health services in urban and suburban settings, patients in rural areas have even more challenges than merely finding a behavioral health care provider. Some locations are so remote that distance is a major obstacle, even when transportation is available. Avera Health is helping to fill this void with eCare Behavioral Health, a telemedicine service that supports clinicians in critical access hospital EDs and acute inpatient units in rural South Dakota, North Dakota, Minnesota, Iowa and Nebraska.

"eCare Behavioral Health provides expert evaluations from mental health professionals via a video camera when a patient with mental health issues arrives in the ED," says Matthew Stanley, DO, clinical vice president of Avera Health's behavioral health service line. Partner sites are provided ahead of time with a mobile cart equipped with all the technology needed to conduct the virtual visit. "Our clinicians can respond to a call for help in 20 minutes or less," Stanley states. "In addition to performing crisis assessments, we engage in

therapeutic interaction. Our clinicians use a collaborative approach to find the most appropriate level of care for each patient, up to and including placement in a psychiatric bed, if necessary." When no beds are available—as is often the case—and a patient must be boarded in the ED, e-health clinicians perform reassessments every 24 hours and manage the patient's medications until a transfer can be made.

Currently, eCare is available in 200 facilities in communities that do not have any mental health care providers. In 2018, when eCare was established, the service logged 3,026 visits. In 2020, because of the COVID-19 pandemic, eCare's patient volume rose exponentially to nearly 4,200 interactions.

"eCare provides 24/7 access to experienced psychiatric staff for patients who would otherwise have to travel hours to be seen by a mental health care provider," Stanley notes. "By reducing ED lengths of stay, improving the continuum of care for patients and supporting local hospital staff, eCare is a critical safety net in communities that are underserved by mental health care providers."

Key Takeaways
Multiple studies have shown that treating behavioral health issues in tandem with medical issues results in better outcomes. Trivedi stresses the

following takeaways in the post-COVID environment:

- **Develop the infrastructure.** By building on whatever behavioral health services their organization already has, health care executives can help move their communities toward a more effective network of mental health services across the spectrum.
- **Create linkages.** Health systems do not need to provide services across the entire continuum. Partnering with providers who are already in this space is a turnkey and cost-effective option.
- **Embrace telehealth.** The pandemic demonstrated that behavioral health services can be effectively delivered via telemedicine, proving it to be a viable alternative to in-person services.

Conclusion
Trivedi cautions that the risks of no action are considerable over time. "Although financial profitability will not necessarily be the outcome of increased investment in behavioral health services, failure to act will result in a negative financial impact downstream through increased hospital readmissions, higher-acuity visits, higher ED boarding levels and worse outcomes for chronic conditions, among other issues. Investing in behavioral health care now will pay great dividends in keeping entire populations healthy for the long term."

References

American Academy of Medical Colleges (AAMC). 2015. "Physician Specialty Data Report: Active Physicians by Age and Specialty, 2015." Accessed May 20, 2021. www.aamc.org/data-reports/workforce/interactive-data/active-physicians-age-and-specialty-2015.

American Psychiatric Association. 2017. "Mental Health Disparities: Diverse Populations." Accessed May 20, 2021. www.psychiatry.org/File%20Library/Psychiatrists/Cultural-Competency/Mental-Health-Disparities/Mental-Health-Facts-for-Diverse-Populations.pdf.

Archer, J., P. Bower, C. Dickens and P. Coventry. 2012. "Collaborative Care for People with Depression and Anxiety." Cochrane. Published October 12. www.cochrane.org/CD006525/DEPRESSN_collaborative-care-for-people-with-depression-and-anxiety.

Bastiampillai, T., S.S. Sharfstein and S. Allison. 2016. "Increase in U.S. Suicide Rates and the Critical Decline in Psychiatric Beds." *Journal of the American Medical Association.* Published December 27. https://jamanetwork.com/journals/jama/fullarticle/2580183.

Bryant, B. 2021. "24% of Health Care CFOs Plan to Divest Their Behavioral Health Operations." *Behavioral Health Business.* Published March 5. https://bhbusiness.com/2021/03/05/24-of-health-care-cfos-plan-to-divest-their-behavioral-health-operations/.

Davenport, S., T.J. Gray and S.P. Melek. 2020. "How Do Individuals with Behavioral Health Conditions Contribute to Physical and Total Healthcare Spending?" Milliman. Published August 13. www.milliman.com/en/insight/How-do-individuals-with-behavioral-health-conditions-contribute-to-physical.

Holland, K.M., C. Jones and A.M. Vivolo-Kantor. 2021. "Trends in U.S. Emergency Department Visits for Mental Health, Overdose, and Violence Outcomes Before and During the COVID-19 Pandemic." *JAMA Psychiatry.* Published February 3. https://jamanetwork.com/journals/jamapsychiatry/fullarticle/2775991.

Merritt Hawkins. 2018. "The Silent Shortage: A White Paper Examining Supply, Demand and Recruitment Trends in Psychiatry." Accessed May 20, 2021. www.merritthawkins.com/uploadedFiles/MerrittHawkins/Content/News_and_Insights/Thought_Leadership/mhawhitepaperpsychiatry2018.pdf.

Substance Abuse and Mental Health Services Administration (SAMHSA). 2020a. "Double Jeopardy: COVID-19 and Behavioral Health Disparities for Black and Latino Communities in the U.S." Published June 11. www.samhsa.gov/sites/default/files/covid19-behavioral-health-disparities-black-latino-communities.pdf.

———. 2020b. "2018 National Survey on Drug Use and Health Detailed Tables: Table 5.38B." Published June. www.samhsa.gov/data/sites/default/files/cbhsq-reports/NSDUHDetailedTabs2018R2/NSDUHDetailedTabs2018.pdf.

Unützer, J., W. Katon, C.M. Callahan, J.W. Williams Jr, E. Hunkeler, L. Harpole, M. Hoffing, R.D. Della Penna, P. Hitchcock Noël, E.H.B. Lin, P.A. Areán, M.T. Hegel, L. Tang, T.R. Belin, S. Oishi, C. Langston and IMPACT Investigators. 2002. "Collaborative Care Management of Late-Life Depression in the Primary Care Setting: A Randomized Controlled Trial." *Journal of the American Medical Association.* Published December 11. https://jamanetwork.com/journals/jama/fullarticle/195599.

How COVID-19 Has Changed Hospital and Health System Emergency Preparedness

with Gregory R. Ciottone, MD

The novel coronavirus pandemic that began in 2019 and continues today with the emergence of more virulent, contagious and resistant variants is the most devastating public health disaster to affect people around the world in more than 100 years. In the United States, which was hit particularly hard in terms of case counts and deaths per capita, hospitals and health systems struggled to manage the surge of patients for most of 2020 and into 2021, with case volumes depending on the effectiveness of nonpharmaceutical interventions (e.g., social distancing, mask wearing), regional rates of vaccinations and compliance with public health directives.

Because of the pandemic, emergency preparedness has become a critically important concern in hospitals and health systems across the country. Shortages of personal protective equipment (PPE), testing equipment, and ventilators; the urgent need to quickly convert hospital wards into intensive care units (ICUs); and a lack of therapeutics to treat COVID-19 early in the pandemic will all inform the response to the next public health catastrophe. Gregory R. Ciottone, MD, director of the division of disaster medicine at Beth Israel Deaconess Medical Center, discusses what hospital and health system leaders should know as we progress through

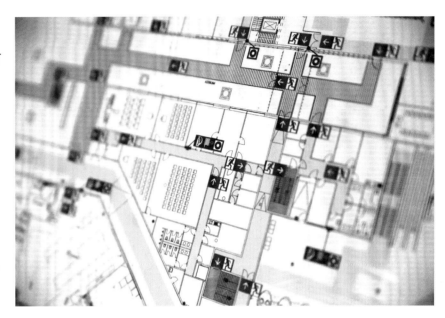

this pandemic and prepare for the next national health emergency.

The Case for Proactive Planning

"Because of COVID-19, we gained a greater understanding of the complexities of disasters. The pandemic has also underscored that we need to pay more attention to emergency preparedness," says Ciottone. "Historically, emergency preparedness has been primarily reactive. To prepare for the next global health crisis, we need to determine more proactively how complex disasters are best mitigated."

While hospitals and frontline care teams have done heroic work in managing the surge in COVID-19 patients, Ciottone believes the overall response to such an overwhelming crisis can clearly be improved. In particular, the nation's handling of the pandemic from a crisis public health perspective lacked foresight, consistent messaging and emergency management. "Any pandemic arising from a novel virus includes a period of time at the beginning when effective therapeutics or vaccines have not yet been developed, necessitating the implementation of nonpharmaceutical

About the Subject Matter Expert

Gregory R. Ciottone, MD, is an emergency physician and the president of the World Association for Disaster and Emergency Medicine. He is the director of the Beth Israel Deaconess Medical Center Fellowship in Disaster Medicine, an associate professor of emergency medicine at Harvard Medical School, and an instructor at the Harvard T.H. Chan School of Public Health. A consultant to the White House Medical Unit, Ciottone is the 2018 recipient of the American College of Emergency Physicians Disaster Medical Services Award and the 2020 recipient of the American Academy of Disaster Medicine Distinguished Service Award.

FUTURESCAN SURVEY RESULTS
Emergency Preparedness

Health care executives from across the nation were asked how likely it is that the following will happen in their hospital or health system by 2027.

By 2027, our hospital or health system will be able to triple its intensive care unit bed surge capacity within a week.

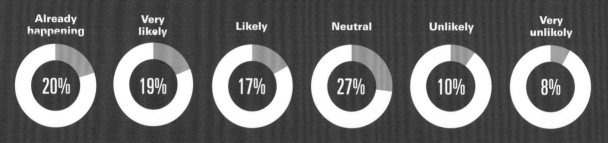

Already happening	Very likely	Likely	Neutral	Unlikely	Very unlikely
20%	19%	17%	27%	10%	8%

By 2027, our hospital or health system will have stockpiles of enough personal protective equipment for one month of peak usage.

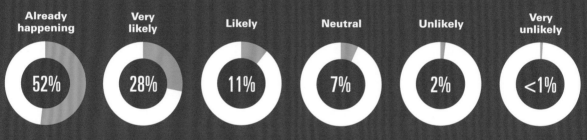

Already happening	Very likely	Likely	Neutral	Unlikely	Very unlikely
52%	28%	11%	7%	2%	<1%

By 2027, our hospital or health system will activate its emergency operations plan at least three times a year (e.g., through an emergency drill or tabletop exercise).

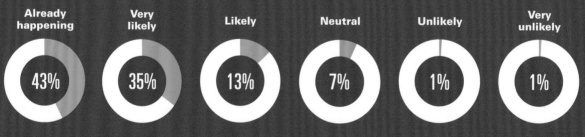

Already happening	Very likely	Likely	Neutral	Unlikely	Very unlikely
43%	35%	13%	7%	1%	1%

Note: Percentages may not sum exactly to 100 percent because of rounding.

interventions (NPIs) that are essentially the only defensive measures we have until lifesaving options become available," he notes. "During the NPI phase of COVID-19, there should have been more consistency and compliance with mask wearing, social distancing, handwashing and other proven measures to protect people from becoming infected." In the future, Ciottone hopes public health and health systems can work together more closely to promote the information required for community understanding of NPIs. He adds, "Broadly, there can always be improvements in plans to handle capacity, address supply chain issues for PPE, increase ICU capabilities and more."

Disaster medicine focuses primarily on surges in patients—whether short-term, such as during a mass casualty event, or long-term, as in the COVID-19 pandemic. "When a sudden influx of patients happens, every medical center should be able to jump from working operations to disaster operations quickly and efficiently," Ciottone says. "Capacity is where it varies—medical centers with 500 beds can respond to a mass casualty event better than small community hospitals can."

Not all communities were prepared for the surge in critical care patients during COVID-19. From a nationwide perspective, Ciottone believes that the overall funding of emergency preparedness at the hospital level should be revisited. The statistics illustrate why: Financial losses in hospitals due to the COVID-19 pandemic are expected to top $323 billion in 2020 (American Hospital Association 2020), whereas only $258 million was appropriated for the Hospital Preparedness Program during the same period (Office of the Assistant Secretary for Preparedness and Response 2020). This figure equates to less than 1 percent of the total U.S. hospital dollar losses projected due to COVID-19 during 2020.

Implications for Health Care Leaders

"Having a disaster plan is important, but that plan will be useful during only the first 10 percent of a crisis," Ciottone states. "This is why I always say, 'Better the planning than the plan.' It is important to prepare for all stages of the disaster cycle: mitigation, which includes the steps taken to lessen the impact of an event; response; recovery; and back to mitigation." In the world of emergency preparedness, Ciottone says, 75 percent of the time and effort is not spent in the response phase but rather in the mitigation, preparedness and recovery phases (exhibit 1), and it includes learning the lessons from the event through an after-action analysis, often referred to as a "hot wash."

Health systems need to be prepared for two types of disasters:

1. **An internal event.** A hospital's reaction to a disaster such as a fire, flood, cyberattack or information technology (IT) shutdown.
2. **An external crisis.** The role a hospital plays as a response asset for the community in the event of a larger disaster outside the medical center campus.

Ciottone stresses that every health care organization should regularly conduct a hazard vulnerability analysis (HVA). In the United States, hospitals are required by the Joint Commission to complete an HVA at least once every year. "HVAs are usually completed by the hospital's emergency manager, in consultation with leadership from various operational and clinical departments," Ciottone states. "In larger medical centers, emergency management committees are common,

Exhibit 1

Disaster Cycle

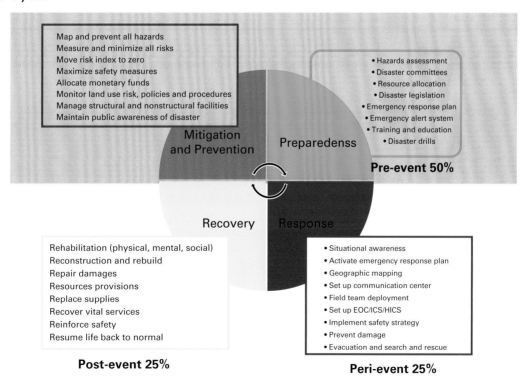

Map and prevent all hazards
Measure and minimize all risks
Move risk index to zero
Maximize safety measures
Allocate monetary funds
Monitor land use risk, policies and procedures
Manage structural and nonstructural facilities
Maintain public awareness of disaster

Mitigation and Prevention

- Hazards assessment
- Disaster committees
- Resource allocation
- Disaster legislation
- Emergency response plan
- Emergency alert system
- Training and education
- Disaster drills

Preparedenss

Pre-event 50%

Rehabilitation (physical, mental, social)
Reconstruction and rebuild
Repair damages
Resources provisions
Replace supplies
Recover vital services
Reinforce safety
Resume life back to normal

Recovery   **Response**

- Situational awareness
- Activate emergency response plan
- Geographic mapping
- Set up communication center
- Field team deployment
- Set up EOC/ICS/HICS
- Implement safety strategy
- Prevent damage
- Evacuation and search and rescue

Post-event 25%   **Peri-event 25%**

Note: EOC = emergency operations center; ICS = incident command system; HICS = hospital incident command system.

with representation from all of these departments."

Comprehensive HVAs consider the emergencies that are most likely to occur from both a historical and a geographic perspective. The outcome of an HVA, called a *relative risk assessment*, should then be used to enhance preparedness for at least 25 percent of the potential emergencies for which the facility is most at risk, according to Ciottone. "For example, if historical precedent and deductive reasoning suggest a hospital is equally likely to experience a flood or earthquake, and the hospital is well prepared for a flood but not a tremblor, then earthquake will be higher on an HVA's output list than flood." An HVA assesses how well prepared a facility is to handle each type of disaster. "HVAs should be guided by emergency management and completed as a team by all in-house stakeholders, including facilities, IT, pharmacy, ICU, nursing and others," Ciottone notes. The resulting disaster plan should then be regularly updated and modified using the HVA.

Ciottone stresses that planning itself is more important than the actual plan. Many hospitals hold annual disaster drills that deploy actual personnel to manage the response, assess the effectiveness and find areas for improvement. A tabletop disaster simulation, where personnel meet to discuss their ideas for an emergency response but do not physically deploy staff and equipment, should incorporate the same problem-solving skills needed during an actual emergency. Tabletop drills allow facilities to prepare for and test disaster plans and operations for large-scale and longer-term events without undertaking a high-fidelity drill. They also allow responders to work through unexpected problems together, thereby anticipating what otherwise may be a surprise in a real event.

Still, planning can accomplish only so much. "During a crisis, events will inevitably take an unexpected trajectory," Ciottone says. "Rarely does a disaster plan apply beyond the initial phase of the crisis. By developing communication channels and practices for working through complex problems during a drill, response stakeholders are developing muscle memory in problem solving. Although no hospital can plan for every single contingency, the planning process will go a long way toward successfully managing an unanticipated disaster."

Ciottone says that some of the problems that emerged during the response to the COVID-19 pandemic were predicted through pandemic influenza tabletop drills performed in facilities across the country over the past decade. "The need for alternate care sites and the ability to repurpose hospital space normally used for elective services are just some of the issues that were identified," he states.

Health care executives have taken the lessons learned from the COVID-19 pandemic to heart. In early 2021, when the most recent *Futurescan* survey was administered, 56 percent said their ability to triple ICU bed surge capacity within one week by 2027 was likely, very likely or already happening. When asked about PPE, more than half (52 percent) of respondents reported that they already had a one-month stockpile, and an additional 28 percent of respondents stated that this would very likely be the case by 2027.

COVID-19 also required implementation of crisis standards of care, when the needs of patients and of the health care workers treating them outstripped assets. "We reach a point where we need to provide the most good to the most people, and rationing becomes necessary," Ciottone explains. "It becomes a matter of adjusting standards of care so more care can be provided to more people." Although crisis standards of care were developed in 2009 during the SARS epidemic, the COVID-19 pandemic was the first time they were considered for widespread implementation.

Ciottone stresses that collaboration and teamwork are critical during a crisis. "Because emergencies rarely take a linear trajectory—whether it's a short-term mass casualty event or a long-term pandemic—it is critical to have working relationships already in place both internally and with outside first responders such as police, fire and state emergency management agencies," Ciottone states. To understand their roles, he recommends gathering response stakeholders together around a

Future emergency preparedness will require a more prominent role not just in health care but in public health and society overall.

preparedness table as often as possible. One emergency that illustrates the value of such preparation prior to a crisis was the Boston Marathon bombing in 2013. "During the response to the bombing, several different agencies worked together on a leadership level as a unified command," Ciottone says. "The response was rapid and effective because the responding agency leaders had a long history of working together, which permitted a team-oriented approach to incident command that resulted in successful crisis leadership. While response agency leaders cannot be expected to have such a level of familiarity with each other in every disaster, the more practice and drills are executed jointly, the more that level of professional comfort can be approximated," Ciottone asserts.

Hospital and health system leaders should view emergency management not as a peripheral function and cost center but rather as essential to quality management and safety. "Emergency preparedness is an investment in overall hospital operations, resulting in process improvements that can positively impact efficiency, care flows and interdepartmental working relationships," Ciottone says. "On further analysis, many of the steps a hospital takes to become more efficient at disaster response are those that also improve overall efficiency and therefore have a positive impact on daily operations." He likens the investment in emergency preparedness to the level of training and simulation that airline pilots undergo on a regular basis. "Pilots spend thousands of hours in training because their lives and those of their passengers depend on them doing the right thing in any conceivable emergency scenario," Ciottone says. "I'd like to see us adopt that same level of preparation in our health care system."

Key Takeaways

Hospitals need to be continually engaged in mitigating, preparing for and responding to complex disasters. Ciottone recommends the following actions:

- **Teach crisis leadership skills.** Crisis leadership requires situational awareness and the understanding that the big picture may not be fully evident early on when events require quick action and the response team to pivot.
- **Ensure every internal department understands its role in a disaster.** Regular HVAs are important, as are internal disaster drills.
- **Maintain relationships with other first responders in the community.** Participate in training with local response agencies, such as large-scale, citywide disaster drills.
- **Establish close linkages with public health agencies to enhance communication and interagency cooperation.** "Working toward better community health education and doing the most good for the most people enhances our collective ability to handle crises," Ciottone stresses.
- **Consider the psychological toll of disasters on health care workers.** "The emotional turmoil of COVID-19 was not anticipated because no one could have imagined the pandemic's magnitude," states Ciottone. "Addressing psychosocial issues proactively should be part of disaster planning in every hospital and health system."

Conclusion

Before the COVID-19 pandemic, hospitals approached emergency preparedness as they had for the past 20 years, but COVID-19 has been a generational event that demonstrated just how devastating a global health crisis can be. As a result, future emergency preparedness will require a more prominent role not just in health care but in public health and society overall. Hospitals can lead the way to ensure we are better prepared for the next global health crisis.

References

American Hospital Association. 2020. "New AHA Report Finds Losses Deepen for Hospitals and Health Systems Due to COVID-19." Published June. www.aha.org/issue-brief/2020-06-30-new-aha-report-finds-losses-deepen-hospitals-and-health-systems-due-covid-19.

Office of the Assistant Secretary for Preparedness and Response. 2020. "ASPR FY 2020 Budget-in-Brief: Public Health and Social Services Emergency Fund." Published August 6. www.phe.gov/about/aspr/Pages/aspr-fy2020-bib.aspx.

ABOUT THE CONTRIBUTORS

Society for Health Care Strategy & Market Development

The Society for Health Care Strategy & Market Development (SHSMD) of the American Hospital Association is the largest and most prominent voice for health care strategists in marketing, strategic planning, business development, communications and public relations. SHSMD is committed to leading, connecting, and serving its members to prepare them for the future with greater knowledge and opportunity as their organizations strive to improve the health of their communities. The society provides a broad and constantly updated array of resources, services, experiences and connections.

SHSMD leaders are available for on-site presentations about *Futurescan 2022–2027* to health care governing boards, senior management, planning teams and medical staffs. To arrange for a leadership presentation, contact SHSMD at 312.422.3888 or shsmd@aha.org.

American College of Healthcare Executives/Health Administration Press

The American College of Healthcare Executives is an international professional society of more than 48,000 healthcare executives who lead hospitals, healthcare systems and other healthcare organizations. ACHE's mission is to advance its members and healthcare leadership excellence. ACHE offers its prestigious FACHE® credential, signifying board certification in healthcare management. ACHE's established network of 77 chapters provides access to networking, education and career development at the local level. In addition, ACHE is known for its magazine, *Healthcare Executive*, and its career development and public policy programs. Through such efforts, ACHE works toward its vision of being the preeminent professional society for leaders dedicated to advancing health.

The Foundation of ACHE is known for its educational programs—including the annual Congress on Healthcare Leadership, which draws more than 4,000 participants—and groundbreaking research. Its publishing division, Health Administration Press, is one of the largest publishers of books and journals on health services management, including textbooks for college and university courses. For more information, visit www.ache.org.